Ethics Embodied

Ethics Embodied

*Rethinking Selfhood through Continental, Japanese,
and Feminist Philosophies*

Erin McCarthy

Foreword by Thomas P. Kasulis

LEXINGTON BOOKS
A division of
ROWMAN & LITTLEFIELD PUBLISHERS, INC.
Lanham • Boulder • New York • Toronto • Plymouth, UK

Published by Lexington Books
A division of Rowman & Littlefield Publishers, Inc.
A wholly owned subsidiary of The Rowman & Littlefield Publishing Group, Inc.
4501 Forbes Boulevard, Suite 200, Lanham, Maryland 20706
http://www.lexingtonbooks.com

Estover Road, Plymouth PL6 7PY, United Kingdom

British Library Cataloguing in Publication Information Available

Library of Congress Cataloging-in-Publication Data

The hardback edition of this book was previously cataloged by the Library of Congress as follows:

McCarthy, Erin, 1969–
  Ethics embodied : rethinking selfhood through continental, Japanese, and feminist philosophies / Erin McCarthy ; foreword by Thomas P. Kasulis.
     p. cm.
  Includes bibliographical references and index.
  1. Philosophy, Japanese. 2. Watsuji, Tetsuro, 1889–1960. 3. Feminist theory. 4. Continental philosophy. 5. Human body. 6. Ethics. I. Title.
  B5242.M33 2010
  170—dc22   2011

                                   2010016844

ISBN: 978-0-7391-2049-1 (cloth : alk. paper)
ISBN: 978-0-7391-2050-7 (pbk. : alk. paper)
ISBN: 978-0-7391-4786-3 (electronic)

∞™ The paper used in this publication meets the minimum requirements of American National Standard for Information Sciences—Permanence of Paper for Printed Library Materials, ANSI/NISO Z39.48-1992.

Printed in the United States of America

For Paul and our daughters, Emma and Kathryn
—my source of unmitigated joy

Contents

Foreword, *Thomas P. Kasulis*   ix

Acknowledgments   xvii

Chapter 1   Introduction   1

Chapter 2   Toward a New Ethical Framework: Watsuji in
             Dialogue with the West   11

Chapter 3   The Embodied Self   33

Chapter 4   Toward an Embodied Ethics of Care   55

Chapter 5   Body, Self and Ethics: Watsuji and Irigaray   73

Chapter 6   Conclusion   95

             Bibliography   107

             Index   113

             About the Author   115

Foreword

Erin McCarthy's *Ethics Embodied* is a breakthrough in cross-cultural thought: it brings multiple traditions into a philosophical conversation that significantly enhances our way of thinking about ethics. Her analysis is not merely additive in the sense that it is not a matter of one insight drawn from one place being added to that from another. Instead, it probes the internal linkage among ideas within both present-day Western feminist ethics and the modern Japanese perspective of Watsuji Tetsurō (1889–1960). McCarthy demonstrates that although these perspectives have not, until now, directly engaged each other, they nonetheless share many insights. Through McCarthy's guidance, we come to see something that was already there, but missed by so many of the dominant ethical theories developed in the West in our post-Enlightenment era.

Erin McCarthy's provocative study in embodied ethics presents itself as a work in "comparative feminist ethics." To appreciate this enterprise and its accomplishments, it is helpful to put that self-description into context. Let us begin with the "comparative" designation. Philosophers undertake comparative (East-West) philosophy in various forms, for various purposes. Sometimes it is hermeneutic in intent: the comparativist interprets the thought of one philosopher by reading it in conjunction with another philosopher, especially one from a culturally distinct tradition. For example, one might compare the idealism of Berkeley with that of a Yogācāra Buddhist thinker having a similar idealist orientation but with important differences. Identifying those differences despite the common ground may help us understand

Berkeley's orientation all the better. A variant of this form of hermeneutic comparison is to help us more clearly understand both philosophers, instead of merely one in light of the other.

In other circumstances, comparative philosophy is constructive and supplemental rather than simply hermeneutical. It is constructive in the sense that it engages a traditional (let us assume Western) philosophical topic such as the problem of free will, the meaning of truth, the function of causality, or the nature of personal identity. Its goal is to bring the analysis further than it has gone before. Yet, this form of comparative philosophy also supplements the Western tradition by bringing to it a new twist such as an added argument, a previously unappreciated distinction, or the analysis of a previously unconsidered example. In this way, philosophy can often progress by an infusion of foreign ideas. Such infusions into West thought are, of course, nothing new. One need only think of the way Arab philosophers adopted Aristotelian thought to spur their own thinking and then Arab and Jewish Aristotelianism in turn brought innovation to later Western European Christian scholasticism. In more particular ways, Chinese Neo-Confucian ideas influenced Leibniz, various Indian philosophies affected both Hegel's and Schopenhauer's systems, Daoism inspired Heidegger, and so forth.

This book undertakes both kinds of comparison. First, its analysis will lead readers to reinterpret some features of the theories by Carol Gilligan, Virginia Held, Luce Irigaray, and Watsuji Tetsurō. Second, this book brings Watsuji's insights into the ethics of care and the role of embodiment in moral action, both being emphases in today's Western feminist philosophy. Through Watsuji, McCarthy is able to bring new terminology and new insights to the constructive philosophical enterprise of embodied ethics in the West. Beyond these two modes of comparative philosophy, however, McCarthy's analysis also works on a deeper, still more sophisticated level. Namely, she uses comparative philosophy to help in developing a different way of ethical *thinking* and not just posing alternative answers to "traditional" problems in the field. In this project, Erin McCarthy's comparative philosophizing is its most pioneering, challenging, creative, and fruitful for further philosophical development.

In much of the so-called mainstream of modern Western ethical philosophy, the assumption has been that ethics defines regulative principles and clarifies moral responsibilities. Erin McCarthy has chosen to draw on my terminology in her discussion, identifying that as an ethics of "integrity" that stresses developing proper external relations among discrete and independently existing individuals. Ethical development is, in this case, chiefly intellectual and contractual; that is, one learns how to think ethically by evaluating situations in terms of principles, norms, and responsibilities. In some feminist ethical philosophies such as the ethics of care, however, Mc-Carthy finds a markedly different approach, more in line of what I have called an ethics of "intimacy." In that approach to ethics, the relations between self and other are presumed to be internal rather than external, the assumption being one of interdependence rather than independence. In other words, in an intimacy context, one finds not discrete entities that need to be connected, but instead, entities that already inherently overlap or are internally linked in some respect. Therefore, rather than forging new relations between discrete individuals, intimacy stresses sensibility to, and responsiveness within, the preexisting interdependence of the field within which those individuals already exist.

In drawing out this feminist approach and its assumptions, McCarthy shows that it involves an emphasis on embodiment, another way in which it deviates from the dominant post-Enlightenment understanding. Once disassociated from the integrity model and its emphasis on the cerebral analysis of ethical maxims and principles, these feminist forms of ethics emphasize an engagement with others that includes the somatic and affective. Irigaray's perspective is especially central to this portion of McCarthy's analysis. To sum up: feminist ethical philosophy cuts against much of the mainstream modernist approach in its emphasis on the somatic, the interdependent, and the affective.

By considering such categories as care, affect, nurturing, responsiveness, and somatic engagement, feminist thinkers have significantly enriched our contemporary Western ethical philosophies. One issue arising from this development is how those feminist insights are specific to gender. In what precise sense is feminist philosophy "feminine"? Why might women philosophers be more sensitive to these issues than men philosophers? This is a point at which McCarthy's cross-cultural philosophizing, specifically her consideration of the ethical philosophy of Watsuji Tetsurō, is especially relevant. What McCarthy convincingly shows is that many themes with which she resonates in feminist ethical thinking are also in the modern Japanese philosophy of Watsuji. In fact, I think it is fair to say that through her reading of Watsuji, McCarthy was able to sharpen her focus on what she finds right in the Western feminist ethics she discusses. In this way, her comparative feminist ethics performs its work in all the senses already discussed.

This accord between Watsuji and the feminist ethical theories is surprising, however, when we think about Watsuji's background. Like Nishida Kitarō (1875–1945), the famous founder of the Kyoto School of Japanese philosophy, Watsuji (1889–1960) is often considered one of the most impressive and influential Japanese philosophers of the twentieth century. Although perhaps not a misogynist, Watsuji—like almost all his male philosophical colleagues in his time—was no feminist either. Nor has his thought influenced any feminist thinkers in the West (at least until now). So, there is no obvious link between the two philosophical traditions. Further, Watsuji's ethical thought—with its emphasis on the somatic, the affective, and the interdependent—is not at all an aberration in the history of Japanese philosophy. He explicitly draws on Buddhist, Confucian, and Nativist/Shintō ideas in explaining his philosophical theories. In those respects, Watsuji's philosophy did not challenge either the mainstream tradition of philosophizing nor sexist thinking in his own culture. If all this is correct, why would the ethical theory of a mainstream male Japanese philosopher with no particular feminist sensitivity seem at times so much like a radically new ethical theory arising from Western feminist philosophy?

I believe a clue is that Watsuji and the feminists share in their critiques a common target, what we can call Western modernist intellectualism. The assumption behind that modernist intellectualism is that truth arises only from detached (affectless, nonperspectival, impersonal, context-free) observation and formal reasoning. Many Western feminist thinkers interested in ethics find this a desiccated approach to morality that diminishes or excludes interpersonal engagement, somatic involvement, and compassionate caring. Modern Western culture has constructed its notion of gender in such a way that these diminished qualities are considered "feminine." So, the call to recover those lost dimensions of "embodied ethics," as McCarthy terms it, naturally arises from the previously marginalized or silenced voice of the Western "feminist philosopher." In Japan, by contrast, many of those values suppressed in the modern West were considered mainstream and traditional when the major influx of Western ideas and values began in the mid-nineteenth century. Japan was almost completely closed off from Western influence from the early seventeenth through the mid-nineteenth centuries. So, it missed the birth of the Western enlightenment, but absorbed its fruits when the West forced itself on Japanese culture through the U.S. gunships of Commodore Perry in 1853. In that era's global politics, Japan—in many respects still a feudal society with little modern Western technology—faced the choice of either being a colony or a colonizer. Opting for the latter alternative, it developed a militant nationalism based in rapid "modernization," a code word for "Westernization."

In its technological development, Japanese society rapidly incorporated scientific thinking with its implicit atomism, scientific observation, and universalistic rational principles. In the areas of ethics and philosophical anthropology, Western ideas of individualism, positivism, scientism, and rationalism entered the culture, overwhelming what had been the Japanese traditional mainstream. The Japanese of Watsuji's generation cut their philosophical teeth by reading Kant, Hegel, the utilitarians, the positivists, and the existentialists. In fact, Watsuji's first three philosophical monographs were on Schopenhauer, Nietzsche, and Kierkegaard. A consequence of this Western impact on Japan was that many intellectuals of the early twentieth century, like many present-day Western feminist philosophers, felt the values central to their identity were being suppressed. For many of the Western feminists this was the problem of reclaiming and taking ownership of the "feminine" virtues that Enlightenment thinking has so thoroughly debased. For the Japanese philosophers, it was one of rediscovering the "Japaneseness" that had been suppressed in their breakneck race toward Western modernity. Watsuji's ethical theories and philosophical anthropology arose in that context.

We must not make the error of taking the context of either feminist ethics or Watsuji's ethics too narrowly, however. Watsuji's "Japanese ethics" is not an ethics only for Japanese any more than the "feminist ethics" discussed in this book is an ethics only for women. Both theories are general theories of ethics based in an understanding of our basic humanity. With the modern Western intellectualization of ethical philosophy, part of that basic humanity has been obscured, denied, and almost erased. In denying either the "feminine" or the "Japanese," we are not denying merely women or the Japanese; we are denying part of what every one of us is. In its most robust form, the common denominator between Watsuji's ethics and feminist ethics—what McCarthy calls "embodied ethics"—is pushing for a better way of ethical thinking that would enhance the lives of all people and all societies.

This is not to ignore cultural difference, gender difference, class difference, or racial difference. Every philosopher, probably every individual, has to figure out where the universal ends and the specific begins. In what sense, I must ask myself, am I a human being, and in what sense a white, male, Anglophone American of the early twenty-first century? Modern Japanese philosophers were acutely aware of the problems involved in defining the relationships among universality, specificity, and individuality.[1] It is crucial, however, that we do not allow our well-placed mistrust of universalization to lead us to deny *all* common elements in our humanity. Let us consider, for example, the nature of the body, a focus in McCarthy's analysis. Although the image, understanding, and performance of the body may be socially constructed, it does not follow the body itself is no more than a social construction. A properly applied tourniquet can save the life of a bleeding victim regardless of that person's gender, culture, class, or race. Also, unfortunately, we can easily design weapons that can kill *any* human being regardless of how that individual might socially construct his or her concept of the body. To put this point bluntly, we live our lives imprinted by specific social and cultural constructions of gender, class, authority, race, and ethnicity, but life itself—in its most primal sense—undergirds those constructions. The more we understand the body in its social constructions, the more we also edge up to that liminal area in which there is universality at the ground of specificity. We can never understand our lives by abstracting our reflections into the universal, but we also can never understand life if we deny our concrete common ground. As I read McCarthy's *Ethics Embodied,* I was repeatedly struck by her skill in explaining the particulars in such a way that triggered insights into the general and individual as well. This is comparative philosophy at its best.

I hope my brief comments help explain my claim that McCarthy's comparative feminist ethics brings a new dimension to our ethical thinking. This book is not really an answer to particular ethical problems, nor a normative prescription for taking certain actions rather than others. The most profound contribution of *Ethics Embodied* is that it highlights and develops a new way of ethical thinking. It is, of course, not completely "new." In some of his writings, Watsuji took pains to explain similarities between his ideas and some aspects of Western ethical theories such as the *ethos-polis* relation in Aristotle or the Kantian notion of "Person." In philosophy perhaps no idea is ever really "new," but rather a rediscovery or reemergence of something almost lost or forgotten. Philosophy is, after all, the "love of wisdom," not knowledge. The knowledgeable person tells us something we did not know; the wise person reminds us of something important that we have forgotten, repressed, or ignored. In that sense, *Ethics Embodied* is philosophical to its core. Erin McCarthy helps us recapture a part of ourselves and of our human relatedness that we might otherwise have missed. We are all indebted to her for sharing her love of wisdom with us, her readers.

Thomas P. Kasulis

Note

1. Watsuji's contemporary, the Kyoto School philosopher Tanabe Hajime (1885–1962) developed, in fact, a sophisticated "logic of the specific" to demarcate a middle ground between the polarities of individual and universal. Another contemporary, Kuki Shūzō (1888–1941), had studied with Heidegger and knew Sartre, but

rejected their philosophical anthropologies for being too individualistic (as *Da-sein*) and too simplistically physicalistic (as *in-der-Welt Sein*). What they both missed, according to Kuki, was an appreciation of how human beings always find themselves in the coloration of their *cultural* time and place, what he called "being of a people" (*minzoku sonzai*).

Acknowledgments

There are many people whose support and encouragement have been instrumental in the writing of this book. My friends, colleagues and students at St. Lawrence University were enormously helpful during the writing process. Eve Stoddard, Marina Llorente, John Collins, Ross Glover, Ken Church, Mary Hussmann, Margaret Bass, Natalia Singer and Karl Schonberg read and responded to much of what appears in the book. Danielle Egan is a valued colleague, interlocutor, critic, reader and supporter of the project from inception to completion—and also the best friend I could ever ask for. My students read and heard bits and pieces of the manuscript over the years, especially those in my Asian and Feminist Philosophy courses, and helped me clarify my ideas.

Bob Carter encouraged me to undertake this project instead of pursuing the safer path of publishing my dissertation. I am extremely grateful for his support and enthusiasm at every stage of the book. I am also grateful to ASIANetwork for a Freeman Student/Faculty Fellows Grant and the Dean's Research Fund of St. Lawrence University which supported my research as a Visiting Scholar at the Nanzan Institute for Religion and Culture. During the writing of this book, I returned several times to the Nanzan Institute and am thankful for their support of the project as well as the continued funding provided by St. Lawrence University. I had many helpful conversations during my stays at Nanzan and would like especially to thank Ben Dorman, Gereon Kopf, Rosemary Morrison, Paul Swanson, and Manabu Watanabe. A debt of gratitude goes to Jim Heisig, who was director during most of my visits, pointed me towards many helpful sources and pushed me to clarify my ideas. And it was at the Nanzan Institute that I first met Tom Kasulis. I am deeply indebted to his work and to him for his support. I am also very grateful to him for writing the foreword to the book.

I would also like to acknowledge the support of the Lenz Foundation for American Buddhism and Naropa University, which awarded me the Lenz Residential Fellowship for Buddhism and American Values, allowing me to spend a semester at Naropa completing the book. I would in particular like to thank those who welcomed me into their community and classrooms and allowed me to see contemplative education in action, particularly Judith Simmer-Brown. And special thanks to Christine Caldwell for the many inspiring conversations which helped me think through the practical possibilities of the philosophy I present here.

Finally I could not have completed this project without the support of my family. I thank Mom and Dad, Scott and Kim, Christa and Justin, for their support and for (almost) never asking, "When is your book going to be done?" To Lisa, Raymond and Jacqueline, for their encouragement, support and the many dinners that helped sustain me. And finally to Paul, for his unflagging support, pushing me to clarify and explain my ideas and for reading the manuscript time and again—I could not have finished this without you.

CHAPTER ONE

Introduction

Ethics Embodied is in many senses introductory—I hope to introduce those interested in Japanese philosophy to feminist philosophies and those interested in feminist philosophies to Japanese philosophy as well as those with an interest in comparative philosophy to another mode of comparison. What follows here opens a dialogue and prepares the way for further exploration of ideas among these disparate and hitherto separated voices as they enter into dialogue with one another.

In this book I engage in comparative feminist philosophy. I compare what may appear at first glance two philosophies that could not be further apart—modern Japanese philosophy and contemporary Western feminist philosophy. To those unfamiliar with the field of comparative feminist philosophy, it might seem an odd undertaking. After all, feminism is a philosophical and political movement that began in the West and has little to do with Japanese thought and culture, and Japanese philosophy has little explicit to do with Western feminism. Indeed it is patriarchal in many ways. In fact, comparing these philosophies was not what I first set out to do. Interested in the emphasis on time in phenomenological explorations of self to the exclusion of the role space had in such explorations, first as an undergraduate and then as a graduate student, I began doing a comparative analysis of the work of Martin Heidegger and Wastsuji Tetsurō.[1] I saw this comparison as being useful for showing how a phenomenologically compelling view of self must include both the spatial and the temporal aspects of self, both the body and the mind, to give a complete picture of being-in-the-world. I was lucky, in fact, to have been able to include Watsuji Tetsurō's work in the dissertation as, at the time, I was told that Asian philosophy was not considered "important" enough, and was not something that would ever get me a job. That challenge overcome, however, I began engaging in what I thought was simply comparative philosophical analysis of these two thinkers. Time and again, however, when I would present my work, people would ask questions that often began "[g]iven your obvious feminist interpretation/approach/analysis." So I began to think about this—yes, I was a feminist and identified myself as such, but I did not consider myself at the time a feminist *philosopher*. So why did these others seem to think I was? Was it just that I was concerned with the body? As I read Luce Irigaray's *This Sex Which Is Not One* with a group of fellow graduate students, it was then that I began to realize that if I wasn't doing comparative feminist philosophy yet . . . I wanted to. As I read more feminist philosophers, I was amazed at the resonances I heard between Irigaray, care ethics, and Watsuji—in the ways they conceptualized self and ethics and included the body in their philosophies. I began to imagine the ways in which these philosophies could support and inform each other and what new concept of self and ethics could come from bringing them together, while at the same time wondering how philosophies that at first glance could not be farther apart, could speak to one another? And so, after the dissertation, when I began my career as a professor, I jumped in, began foregrounding what had, unbeknownst to me, always been in the background of my work, and left much, though not all, of the dissertation behind. This book is the result.

As I continued reading more feminist philosophers concerned with ethics and the body I kept recalling themes of Japanese philosophy and Buddhism—wherein we find nondualistic ways of thinking about ethics and the self, ways of thinking that can provide responses to the issues and problems raised by feminist philosophers. Why, I wondered, especially in a time of globalization, had no one turned to this rich resource as a way of bridging cultures and expanding horizons? Perhaps women had to struggle too hard to be accepted seriously doing feminist philosophy, to consider bringing in Asian philosophy? Perhaps both feminist philosophy and Asian philosophy were marginal enough without mixing them? Or, perhaps these two philosophical voices, neither considered mainstream philosophies in many departments, simply had not met before. And so in a sense, this book could not have been written until this particular moment in time.

The book goes beyond comparative analysis, however. As feminist philosophy arises out of a political movement, I am unabashed about also having a political agenda. I hope, in my work, to promote a sense of self that I believe can provide a place for respecting difference—be it between genders, cultures or religions—while respecting and honoring and enacting the deep interconnectedness of all human beings.

A Heuristic Framework

After I had finished the majority of this book, I read Thomas Kasulis's *Intimacy or Integrity*. There, Kasulis proposes a way of thinking about different ways of relating, understanding and being-in-the-world that further dialogue across cultures. Kasulis deftly captures an aspect of what I had been struggling to articulate about what had moved me to undertake the comparative work I was doing, bringing together modern Japanese philosophy with Western feminism. Examining his theory will help make sense of how and why I have chosen to approach this investigation of what it is to be an embodied ethical human being-in-the-world through bringing these philosophies together.

Kasulis suggests that cultures have one of two general orientations of being-in-the-world—an intimacy orientation or an integrity orientation. He acknowledges, though, that it "is unlikely that any culture is ever a perfect example of either an intimacy-dominant or integrity-dominant culture (generalities always have qualifications or exceptions)."[2] In other words, no one culture is ever purely intimacy *or* integrity oriented—his framework allows that the opposite orientations may be present in subcultures even when one orientation dominates. But still, the framework brings to light things which we may not have otherwise noticed, and his "hope is that the analysis and critical tools presented . . . may help us see connections and differences we might have otherwise missed."[3]

On Kasulis's analysis, Western philosophy—its concepts of selfhood, identity and ethics especially, are integrity oriented. To briefly summarize, an integrity-oriented culture views

1. Objectivity as a matter of public verifiability
2. External relations as more fundamental than internal relations
3. Knowledge as ideally empty of affect
4. The intellectual and psychological as distinct from the somatic (the body)
5. Knowledge as reflective and self-conscious of its own grounds[4]

This is the orientation that underlies the emphasis of much modern Western philosophy—a focus on the rational, autonomous, independent individual as the starting point for ethics.

Intimacy-oriented cultures, by contrast, look very different. They stress values which are often found in Asian philosophy, and in some versions of feminist philosophy. According to intimacy-oriented cultures,

1. Intimacy is objective, but personal rather than public.
2. In an intimate relation, self and other belong together in a way that does not sharply distinguish the two.
3. Intimate knowledge has an affective dimension.
4. Intimacy is somatic as well as psychological.
5. Intimacy's ground is not generally self-conscious, reflective, or self-illuminating.[5]

While the dominant paradigm of modern Western philosophical culture is clearly the integrity-based model, there are, as Kasulis recognizes, subcultures within this dominant culture that are intimacy based. For example, we find this orientation in feminist philosophy, in the work of Carol Gilligan and Nel Noddings[6] and French philosopher Luce Irigaray, for example—each of whom engages in an intimacy-based way of philosophizing. As we will see in more detail in the chapters that follow, both philosophies view self as relational, and Irigaray includes the body as a constituting aspect of selfhood. In what follows, unless otherwise specified, I read the body as that through and in which we experience life and the world, as that which integrates thought and feeling and the experience of the world around us. The body is *not* an object, is not separate from mind or self. The body, or in fact the self is, as I maintain both Irigaray and Watsuji would agree, what we might call a complex, or "bodymind"[7] as in the Japanese tradition, one that encompasses mind and body as "interdependent facets of a single phenomenon."[8] And yet, each one of these phenomena is also unique, and to be embodied male or female, black or white, rich or poor has very real, material, immediate consequences.[9] That we find this intimacy orientation in feminist philosophy is not surprising, for as Kasulis points out, in "a patriarchal society . . . men would be taught to focus on the dominant [integrity] orientation and this would leave the other orientation for the women. In this way, the societal structure reinforces the patriarchy by giving the male-defined roles more cultural authority."[10] However, Kasulis also points out that the *intimacy*-oriented approach is the dominant one in Japanese philosophy and the *integrity* orientation forms a subculture. Viewed from within his analysis then, it is not surprising that I found myself exploring resonances between Japanese philosophy and Western feminist philosophy. Thus Kasulis's heuristic provides one explanation as to why there are strong resonances in the way selfhood and ethics are conceptualized in these two seemingly completely different cultures.

Kasulis's theory also gives further support to my comparative project when he points out that however much any traditions, such as Japanese and feminist philosophy, for example, might seem to be completely mutually unintelligible, that this is not in fact entirely the case. As he puts it: "To perceive the other to be 'different' requires a basic understanding grounded in a shared logic. Otherwise I would have no basis for knowing that I do not understand the other. I have to understand the other well enough to know I am not fully understanding the other."[11]

So there is something that does tie these philosophies together across history and cultural and philosophical traditions—an intimacy-oriented approach to philosophy. An embodied ethics seeks to recognize the complex interdependence of human relations—the connections that include but also go beyond both the psychological and corporeal—in our daily lives in a way that has not been recognized in the context of "traditional" or integrity-dominant ethics.

There are differences between the philosophies, to be sure, and it is quite certain that Watsuji had no notion of feminist philosophy and came out of a very male-dominated philosophical and cultural system; but nonetheless I shall urge that there are resonances in his work with the ethics of care and the philosophy of Luce Irigaray that can be explained by having the orientation of intimacy in the background to use as a framework for analysis and cross cultural philosophizing—to help explain why and where these two at first glance opposite cultures meet and resonate, why we can talk across difference here and why each might find philosophical support for its ideas in the other culture.

It is important to also note that none of the philosophies I engage with in the book are examples of a pure intimacy orientation. Watsuji's philosophy, while coming out of a predominantly intimacy-oriented culture, is firmly rooted in the context of a patriarchal Japan and so has a strong integrity thread running through it, and the feminist philosophies I engage with, having developed out of integrity-oriented cultures themselves, are, not surprisingly, concerned with retaining a sense of autonomy for the self even within the intimacy-oriented philosophies that they develop. What Kasulis's theory supports is that despite differences, there is a ground for understanding across difference. The comparative work I engage in here seeks to develop a concept of self which would not just include, but embody, philosophical empathy: the other is, after all, not entirely incomprehensible; there is something we understand about her, even if we might not "get" what she is trying to say.

Unfortunately, it is the enacting of philosophical empathy where we often go wrong—in personal relationships, in the classroom, in world affairs—when cross cultural dialogue gets difficult or when an encounter with another culture or another person reveals something about our own culture or self that we may not be willing to face. Particularly in an integrity-dominant culture, the temptation, when communication gets difficult, when caring or loving becomes challenging, the easy way out, and what we see time and again, regardless of philosophical or cultural orientation, is the tendency to frame differences in terms of "us versus them," or "you versus me." Even in the intimacy orientation, we have "insider versus outsider," wherein the intimacy group seeks to protect the members of its group from outsiders.[12] Either way, when we construe the relationship with the other in oppositional terms as some sort of a clash of civilizations or cultures, we are virtually guaranteeing that communication will fail and that there will be no place for ethics. Engaging in the sort of comparative feminist philosophy I pursue here seeks to keep open the space of philosophical empathy, to create a concept of self that is open to the other, relational and fluid, in other words, intimate, but not at the expense of autonomy or integrity. This concept of self that I ultimately aim to develop, Kasulis would call "culturally bi-orientational."[13] This ethical embodied self that develops from my comparative feminist philosophical exploration will then, to use Kasulis's vocabulary, be predominantly intimacy oriented, yet I seek to retain key aspects of integrity oriented cultures, such as autonomy of the self, which is vital when we think about the real lives of women in the world and the variety of ways in which their autonomy has been denied.

Outline of the Book

In chapter 2, I introduce the philosophy of Watsuji Tetsurō (1889–1960). Watsuji was a comparative philosopher of sorts himself. He engaged deeply with Western philosophy, particularly the phenomenological tradition. In this chapter I introduce the main concepts of his ethical theory of the human being as *ningen*. For the reader unfamiliar with Japanese philosophy, I look at Watsuji's philosophy in comparison with Heidegger and Husserl. In comparing Watsuji with Heidegger, I show how Heidegger, while he sought to avoid the mistakes of Cartesian dualism, still falls into many of the same traps, particularly that of the isolated individual. In *Being and Time*, for Watsuji at least, Heidegger's phenomenological analysis only gives us part of what it is to be a human being-in-the-world due to his lack of analysis of the spatial aspect of human being. I then turn to the philosophy of Husserl, where we do find more in common with Watsuji, given Husserl's concept of intersubjectivity. Even here however, the comparison will reveal that Husserl does not go far enough, that, when compared to Watsuji's concept of self as *ningen*, even Husserl's intersubjectivity falls short, with each subject still trapped by and in his or her own subjectivity, unable to fully bridge the gap between self and other.

Chapter 3 focuses on the body in self and ethics. I begin by looking at the body in Husserl's phenomenology and show how, on Watsuji's view, despite the fact that Husserl at least takes account of the body in his philosophy, that he still remains trapped in a dualistic view which prevents him from giving a satisfying account of the body. I then articulate feminist critiques of the Western philosophical traditions to show how they resonate with the critiques of the ethics and the role of the body brought to bear on Western philosophy in Watsuji's and one of his last students, Yuasa Yasuo's (1925–2005) work. Next I continue the discussion of *ningen* begun in chapter 2, focusing in this chapter on the connection between *ningen*, ethics, and the body. To further flesh out Watsuji's perspective, I also discuss some Zen Buddhist ideas that are in the background of many of Watsuji's concepts, through the analysis done by Yuasa. I show how Japanese philosophy has a nondualistic view of the body, in contrast to the way the body has been viewed in much of ancient and modern Western philosophy. In the Japanese philosophy that I will discuss, body is fully integrated in any conceptualization of self as much as mind is. Understanding the relationship between self, body and ethics in Watsuji provides the foundation for the comparisons with feminist philosophies to come in chapters 4 and 5.

Still working with the themes and concepts discussed thus far, chapters 4 and 5 foreground two different feminist philosophies—care ethics and the philosophy of Luce Irigaray. In chapter 4, I explore the resonance between Watsuji's notion of self as *ningen* and the notion of self found in feminist ethics of care drawing mainly on the work of Virginia Held. Here we see Kasulis's theory of intimacy-oriented philosophies illustrated most clearly. I bring together Japanese and feminist philosophies, incorporating each into the other. I argue that Watsuji's thought provides proponents of care ethics with rich ways of thinking about the self that are inherently nondualistic, that resist the mind/body split. At the same time, I insist this comparative approach to an ethics of care remains a feminist project. I will demonstrate how each framework of self and ethics can support, inform and enrich the other, bringing to light strengths and weaknesses to be kept in mind in each philosophy.

Chapter 5 may at first seem to be the most unlikely pairing in this comparative exploration—Watsuji's philosophy and the work of French feminist philosopher, Luce Irigaray. In this chapter I pursue Irigaray's suggestion in her 2002 book *Between East and West*, that we turn to Asian philosophies for frameworks other than those provided by Western philosophy to re-imagine woman's subjectivity. I apply her suggestion to her own work, and suggest that in addition to the Indian philosophy that she has explored, that if we can make a case for Irigaray's philosophy operating on an intimacy-based orientation, then her philosophy resonates even more strongly, in my view, with that of Watsuji. Each proposes, on my reading, a nondualistic concept of selfhood that changes the way we think about both self and ethics.

Taking my cue from the praxis aspects inherent in both Japanese and feminist philosophies, in the final chapter I look ahead to practical applications of the kind of ethical, embodied selfhood for which I have been arguing. I explore the possibility of integrating the theory and practice of contemplative education in the liberal arts classroom as one way in which this kind of selfhood can be cultivated.

Notes

1. Japanese names are written using the Japanese convention of family name, followed by first name.

2. Thomas P. Kasulis, *Intimacy or Integrity: Philosophy and Cultural Difference* (Honolulu: University of Hawaii Press, 2002), 11.

3. Kasulis, *Intimacy*, 11.

4. See Kasulis, *Intimacy*, 25 and also 53–70.

5. Kasulis, *Intimacy*, 25.

6. Kasulis himself points this out in his intimate bibliography (*Intimacy*, 161–179). There has been much written on the body recently in various areas of philosophy—in Asian philosophy (see for example: *Self as Body in Asian Theory and Practice*, ed. Thomas P. Kasulis with Roger T. Ames and Wimal Dissanayake (Albany: SUNY Press, 1993), *The Body: Toward an Eastern Mind-Body Theory*, Yuasa Yasuo, ed. Thomas P. Kasulis, trans. Nagatomo Shigenori and Thomas P. Kasulis (Albany: SUNY Press, 1987), *The Bodymind Experience in Japanese Buddhism: A Phenomenological Study*, David Edward Shaner (Albany: SUNY Press, 1985)), in feminist philosophy (for example, two very influential books in this field were *Bodies That Matter*, Judith Butler (New York: Routledge, 1993) and *Volatile Bodies*, Elizabeth Grosz (Bloomington: Indiana U.P., 1994)), and of course in phenomenology (for example, *The Visible and the Invisible*, Maurice Merleau-Ponty, ed. Claude Lefort, trans. Alphonso Lingis (Evanston: NorthWestern 1968)). However, while phenomenologists, feminist and Asian philosophers have addressed the body and its place in ethics and selfhood, they have yet to speak to one another in the ways I propose here.

7. David Edward Shaner, *The Bodymind Experience in Japanese Buddhism: A Phenomenological Study of Kūkai and Dōgen* (Albany: SUNY Press, 1985), 45.

8. Thomas P. Kasulis, "The Body—Japanese Style," in *Self as Body in Asian Theory and Practice*, ed. Thomas P. Kasulis with Roger T. Ames and Wimal Dissanayake (Albany: SUNY Press, 1993), 305.

9. Tamsin Lorraine, *Irigaray and Deleuze: Experiments in Visceral Philosophy* (Ithaca: Cornell U.P., 1999), 1–2. See the introduction to this book, where Lorraine problematizes and sets up the problem of how to take the body into account in philosophy with great skill and nuance. It is also interesting to note that while she does not take it up, also in the introduction Lorraine hints at the connection between Irigaray and Japanese philosophy in footnote 8 referring to the work of Yuasa, stating, "[T]he approach of Yuasa toward mind/body dualisms . . . is in keeping with the kind of approach I advocate here" (241).

10. Kasulis, *Intimacy*, 138.

11. Kasulis, *Intimacy*, 136.

12. See Kasulis, *Intimacy*, 147–148.

13. Kasulis, *Intimacy*, 156–157.

CHAPTER TWO

Toward a New Ethical Framework
Watsuji in Dialogue with the West

Long before Merleau-Ponty critiqued Heidegger's treatment of the body, Japanese philosopher Watsuji Tetsurō responded to the lack of the body and the spatial in Heidegger's work. Watsuji was a contemporary of the Kyoto School of Japanese philosophy's founder Nishida Kitarō (1870–1945); however, he is generally considered to be on the fringes of the Kyoto School. As I mentioned in the introduction, I see Watsuji as somewhat of a comparative philosopher. He was schooled in the Western philosophical tradition and particularly interested in phenomenology—his graduating thesis for Tokyo Imperial University was on Schopenhauer—and he was also deeply interested the work of Nietzsche and Kierkegaard, publishing work on each of these philosophers. But Watsuji was also equally interested in Japanese thought and Buddhism and in fact, is the philosopher responsible for reviving interest in the medieval Zen monk and philosopher Dōgen with his *Shamon Dōgen* published in the series *Nihon seishinshi kenkyû* (*A Study of the History of the Japanese Spirit*) the first volume appearing in 1925 and the second in 1935. In 1925, Nishida invited Watsuji to teach ethics at Kyoto University and during this time, he also published *Kirisutokyû no bunkashiteki igi* (*The Significance of Primitive Christianity in Cultural History*), and *Genshi Bukkyō no jissen tetsugaku* (*The Practical Philosophy of Primitive Buddhism*).[1] During a trip to Germany in 1927, Watsuji read *Being and Time*: "I found myself intrigued," he wrote, "by the attempt to treat the structure of man's existence in terms of time but I found it hard to see why, when time had thus been made to play a part in the structure of subjective existence, at the same juncture space also was not postulated as part of the basic structure of existence."[2] It was spending time in Europe and reading *Being and Time* that spurred Watsuji to reflect more deeply on the unique qualities of Japanese thought. After first being drawn to the existentialist view of the self as expressed in the work of Kierkegaard, Schopenhauer and Nietzsche, after the trip to Europe and reading *Being and Time* he began to take a more critical view of the emphasis on the individual self. Upon his return from Europe he began writing *Fūdo* or *Climate and Culture* (written in 1929 but published in 1935), in reaction to the lack of the spatial in *Being and Time*.[3] On Watsuji's analysis, Heidegger's sole focus on temporality meant that he considered only one aspect of human being-in-the-world—the individual. For without taking spatiality into account, Heidegger would not be able to come up with a satisfying account of relationships among and between people—not only the space of their relationships, but also the spaces in which they lived and interacted. Watsuji's larger work, *Rinrigaku* (*Ethics*), which I will focus mostly on here, can be read as a further critique of Western individualism. In this chapter, I first discuss Watsuji's notion of human being as *ningen*, which, unlike Heidegger's Da-sein, includes both the temporal and spatial aspects of human being-in-the-world, and his concept of ethics as the study of human beings (*ningengaku*). I go on to discuss Watsuji's critical appropriation of Heideggerian and Husserlian philosophy. We will first see how Heidegger's Da-sein remains as isolated as Descartes' *cogito* as its foundation is temporal, a being toward-death, which Watsuji in his concept of *ningen* seeks to avoid. I then turn to the philosophy of Husserl, where we do find more in common with Watsuji, given Husserl's concept of intersubjectivity. Even here however, the comparison will reveal that Husserl does not go far enough, that, when compared to Watsuji's concept of self as *ningen*, even Husserl's intersubjectivity falls short, with each subject still trapped by and in his or her own subjectivity, unable to fully bridge the gap between self and other. Juxtaposing Watsuji's view of self as *ningen*, with Heidegger's Da-sein and Husserl's concept of intersubjectivity creates a space to envision an alternative framework for thinking about being-in-the-world—a framework that works toward our critical amalgamation of Japanese and Western feminist concepts of self in an attempt to provide a fuller response to thinking about ethics, self and body. Furthermore, as we will see in chapters 4 and 5, elucidating Watsuji's concept of self and body here paves the way for the later comparisons with feminist philosophies of care ethics and Irigaray's philosophy.

Ethics and the Human Being as Ningen (人間)

"The essential significance of the attempt to describe ethics as the study of *ningen* consists in getting away from the misconception, prevalent in the modern world, that conceives of ethics as a problem of individual consciousness *only*."[4] So opens Watsuji's *Ethics*. Here we see that Watsuji takes issue with the Western philosophical tradition's approach to ethics, in particular its individualistic concept of self. On Wastuji's analysis, Western philosophy's view of self has been of a self that possesses an identity that is intrinsic to it and is only contingently related to other human beings. The core of Wastuji's ethical theory is his concept of human being understood as *ningen*. The locus of ethical problems, he tells us, "lies not in the consciousness of the isolated individual, but precisely in the in-betweenness of person and person."[5] In other words, ethics is the study of human beings, or *ningengaku* (人間学): human beings not only as individual but also as social in the betweenness (*aidagara* 間柄) among selves in the world. For him, there is no characterization of individuality applicable to selves that can be understood without consideration of that individual's relations to others. His definition of human being as *ningen* includes self not only as *both* individual and relational, but also as embodied, for these relations between people, as we will see in detail in chapter 3, are not merely relations between minds, but between embodied human beings. Watsuji's concept of human being as *ningen* is at odds with the Western concept of self as *purely* individual, where relationships with others are only contingent. The very terms used to designate self—*homo, man, mensch*—he argues, indicate that self, in the West, is conceived of in terms of the isolated individual. Such a concept, he argues, is merely an abstraction, for as *ningen*, we are always in relation with other human beings. The Japanese word *ningen* is composed of the characters for person, 人, and between, 間, signifying the individual and social *at the same time*. It is "the public, and, at the same time, the individual human beings living within it. . . . What is recognizable here is a dialectical unity of those double characteristics that are inherent in a human being."[6] Taken literally then, as *ningen*, self is "between persons" which is actually a very helpful way to think about this concept, for *ningen* is not really a thing but more like a place or space, but not a fixed place either. It is more like a shifting network of relations being configured and reconfigured in time and space.

Ningen is a dynamic concept of self, one that John Maraldo has suggested be understood, not as a metaphysical entity, rather as an interrelation.[7] *Ningen* is not to be understood as something fixed with a determinate identity; rather, as *ningen*, one's identity is found relationally—between persons—and as such continually shifts and changes. Indeed to be *ningen* means to move freely between the social and individual. For Watsuji, to be human, to be *ningen*, is also to be ethical and one cannot be either unless one is both an individual—different from others—and yet also *at the same time*, in relation with others. As Maraldo puts it, for "Watsuji the concrete reality of being human lies in the midst of the two more abstract poles, the individual and the social."⁸ *Ningen* "although being subjective communal existence as the interconnection of acts, at the same time, is an individual that acts through these connections. This subjective and dynamic structure does not allow us to account for *ningen* as a 'thing' or 'substance.'"⁹ Because part of what it means to be *ningen* is to be dynamic, it cannot be thought of as a stable or final or completed object or thing. To be sure, *ningen* is an individual, but *ningen* is also at the same time "subjective communal existence."¹⁰ This "at the same time" is key and expresses the nonduality of *ningen*. One is not first an individual and then in relation; nor is it the case that one is *either* an individual *or* in relation. Rather *ningen* is *both* an individual *and* in relation at the same time, and to isolate either of these two aspects of being human, for Watsuji, does not express the fullness of what it is to be a human being. To explain it using Kasulis's model, as *ningen*, "my identity in the intimacy orientation . . . necessarily overlaps with what is outside the discrete ego."¹¹ *Ningen* transcends dualities and defies what we might normally think of as self. There is no self substance, for example, no idea of "soul" at play here. *Ningen* has, as part of its structure, a refusal to be a self-containing, self-contained object; its very structure is nondualistic. As William Lafleur explains:

> according to Watsuji, both sides of human existence, man's existence as an individual and his existence as society, are *coequal* and thought of as such. The important point is that the notion of being in relationship is not secondary or an afterthought but, along with the individuated aspect, constitutive of man *from the outset.*¹²

Moreover, Watsuji's definition of human being as *ningen*, as we will see in depth in the next chapter, includes self not only as coequally individual and relational, but also as embodied.

Watsuji's nondualistic concept of self stands in sharp contrast to most Western notions of self, which are dualistic. For the purposes of this study, a view is dualistic if it conceives of the self in terms of the dichotomies of mind and body, self and other, and so on. Dualists locate the self in some subset of the elements of human being (such as reason, individual consciousness, the brain, or an individual soul) and view these core elements as more authentically human than the others and thereby worthy of more weight, authority or value. On such a view, cultivation of these elements of the self is essential to becoming fully human in a way that the development of the other elements is not. This sort of view takes the remaining elements to be, if not inimical to human development, at best ancillary to it. Examples of dualist conceptions of self span various metaphysical and ontological commitments regarding the self. Ontological dualism is a clear example of this, since it involves the separation of mind from body—but physicalists can be, and often are, equally dualists in my sense. It is worth noting that dualism need not imply a rationalist conception of the self—someone who pits passion against reason is no less dualistic than someone who pits reason against passion. And while individualism is a dualistic view—since it views the ethical self as prior to and separate from its communal roles—to take communal relations to be fundamental to selfhood and individuality as a pernicious abstraction is also a dualistic view in my sense.

Nondualism, on the other hand, rejects the sharp distinctions between body and mind, self and other, and subject and object. In each case, it is a matter of both/and, rather than either/or. That is, nondualism allows for difference to be retained even as it is transcended. On this view, self is constituted by both mind and body at the same time, yet neither is more important or fundamental to the ethical self than the other. Similarly, and for the philosophers examined here in particular, a nondualistic concept of self views each person's ethical identity as integrally related to that of others. Mind and body, self and other, are viewed as inseparable from ethical identity related to, rather than viewed as opposed to, or exclusive of, each other.

In Watsuji's *ningen*, we find this nondualism lived out. A fundamental aspect of *ningen* is the movement of transcending dualities; of dissolving of individual into community, of self into other, and back again and somehow all of this at the same time, and has its roots in the Buddhist notion of emptiness or nothingness—*ku*.[13] One aspect of this influence is the role of negation and emptiness in the concept of *ningen* which we will look at briefly here to better understand its role in Watsuji's ethics and return to in chapter 5.

The notion of self-negation and contradiction is one of the most complex in Watsuji's philosophy and in this idea we hear echoes of Nishida's philosophy. For Watsuji, one is not fully human nor ethical until one acknowledges the tension between the individual and social aspects of *ningen* and the necessity of continuing to move between the two poles, that is, negating the individual (collapsing the difference between self and other) and negating the social and so on.[14] As he puts it, "the negative structure of a betweenness-oriented being is clarified in terms of the self-returning movement of absolute negativity through its own negation."[15] Watsuji's talk of self in terms of constant negating of negation might sound nihilistic—or a denial of any positive notion of self. In fact, it is anything but. While his notion of self is not fixed, he conceives the self as something rich and dynamic and, contrary to nihilism, as fundamentally linked to others even while at the same time being distinct from them. We can relate this notion of emptiness in Watsuji's *ningen* and the negation we find in his philosophy to the Mahayana Buddhist notion of dependent co-origination.[16] Dependent co-origination means that everything is intricately interconnected and thus, that the idea of independent existence—of anything at all, including the self—is in fact, empty, so ultimately our relatedness is one of self-lessness. As Carter explains it, "everything is deprived of its substantiality, nothing exists independently, everything is related to everything else, nothing ranks as a first cause, and even the *self* is but a delusory construction. The delusion of independent individuality can be overcome by recognizing our radical relational interconnectedness. At the same time, the negation must be negated, so our radical relational interconnectedness is possible only because true individuals have created a network in the betweenness between them."[17] If we apply this to Watsuji's structure of *ningen*, the betweenness itself is *ku*, or emptiness, and provides the ground for the interconnectedness or interdependence of *ningen*. It is what Kasulis would refer to as part of *ningen*'s internal relations. In other words, in the intimacy orientation that is part of *ningen*, its relatents are part of its identity—where self and other interrelate is betweenness or *ku*, emptiness.[18] We can then see how, out of co-dependent origination emerges, as mentioned above, the notion of no-self, which we can also see reflected in Watsuji's *ningen*. The Buddhist belief is that there is no permanent, abiding self. For practical purposes we may identify our "selves" as such, but a closer examination reveals that in fact there is no *permanent* self—what we normally consider to be permanent, as having independent existence, is also illusory and but a construction. As we have seen, Watsuji's *ningen* is also constantly in flux, never fixed or permanent, continually moving between the poles of individual and social and this is a fundamental aspect of *ningen*. In chapter 5 we will see how this fluid or "empty" notion of selfhood resonates with Irigaray's philosophy and how such fluid or "empty" concepts of self make it easier to meet in the betweenness precisely because they begin with a considerably weaker notion of self than we are accustomed to in most traditional Western philosophy.

Ningen is then, "a betweenness-oriented being."[19] Watsuji identifies three moments that the negation or emptiness inherent in being *ningen* encompasses: "fundamental emptiness, then individual existence, and social existence as its negative development. These three are interactive with one another in practical reality and cannot be separated. They are at work constantly in the practical interconnection of acts and can in no way be stabilized fixedly at any place."[20] Even though, as Watsuji himself states, these three moments are constantly interactive with each other and inseparable,

I will try to elucidate what he means by each. Let's start with the individual existence—for Watsuji, we recall, the individual has no determinate identity in herself. As he puts it: "Individual persons do not subsist in themselves."[21] Rather, as we know, individual persons exist in the between. *Ningen*, as we have seen, is interdependent, so the idea of the "individual," isolated human being is in fact, empty. Yet, the individual does exist, by negating the group, by distinguishing itself from the other members with whom it exists in the between, by stepping away from the group. One defines oneself as separate or apart from the group, as distinct from it. Think of a teenager establishing his own identity by pushing away, separating himself from his parents, for example. However, this very movement of the establishing of the individual which negates the group *at the same time* admits that there *is* a group or rela-tion to which one belongs. So, the *individual* is negated in this very act of establishing himself because he admits that he is also a part of the group, part of the between, which negates his individual existence.

There is, however, another aspect of emptiness at work here—which grounds *ningen*—the fundamental emptiness that exists in the between, where self and other cease to exist, where the dualism of subject and object is overcome. This notion of fundamental emptiness at play here comes out of the tradition of Mahayana Buddhism. In fact, Isamu Nagami points out that the very word *ningen* has its origins in Buddhism: "*Ningen* was originally a Buddhistic word and was placed in between *chikushō-kai* (the place where bird, beasts, fishes, worms and other creatures belong to the subhuman spe-cies) and *tenjō-kai* (heaven). Within this Buddhistic world-view, [Watsuji] points out that *ningen* can be understood at *yono-naka*. . . . (to be in the world)."[22] In Mahayana Buddhism, emptiness is not a nihilistic idea. Rather, it is at the root of everything that exists; it is beyond even the dualism of individual and social. As Kasulis puts it: "Emptiness—the logical interdepen-dence of opposing terms—lies at the basis of all philosophical distinctions,"[23] the particular distinctions here being individual and community. This is the "fundamental emptiness" that Watsuji refers to above and is the place of ethics. As Robert Carter explains, "[t]rue *authenticity* is not the asserting of one's individuality, as with the Existentialists, but an annihilation of the self such that one is now identified with others in a nondualistic merging of self and other."[24] This is both wholeness *and* fundamental emptiness, for just as the individual does not subsist in herself, nor does the whole subsist in itself, but, as Watsuji explains, the whole "appears only in the form of the restric-tion or negation of the individual."[25] To go back to Carter's explanation: "The absolute wholeness [fundamental emptiness] of which Watsuji writes consists of the nonduality of the self and other"; we, and all things, on this

Buddhist view, arise coemergently out of this emptiness "that is the ground of all distinctions, yet that itself is without distinction."[26]

Ningen continually acts out or performs this double movement of negation of the individual and the social. What is particularly interesting is that this process of becoming never comes to a standstill if one is being *ningen*. If the process does stop, betweenness collapses; if it continues however, "the movement of the negation of absolute negativity is, at the same time, the continuous creation of human beings."[27] Watsuji maintains that this is the fundamental structure of our existence as ethical human beings—in other words we are constantly, if we are being fully human, becoming. We are always influencing the world and people we come into contact with and the world and people we are in the between with are influencing our individual selves. The mutual and constant emptying and filling in the act of double negation are at the heart of this way of conceptualizing the self. Self and other, individual and social are unified *yet not fixed* by *ningen*:

> Each of us is both one and many, both an individual as isolated *and* inextricably interconnected with others in some community or other. As *ningen*, we negate our individuality to the extent that we are communally connected, and we negate our communality to the extent that we express our individuality. We are both, in *mutual* interactive negation, as well as being determined by the group or community, *and* determining and shaping the community. As such, we are living self-contradictions and therefore living identities of self-contradiction, or unities of opposites, in mutual interactive negation.[28]

Despite the centrality of the notion of negation, Watsuji's study of the human being-in-the-world is anything but nihilistic. In fact, as Carter argues, precisely as a result of the double negation inherent in *ningen*, there is a ground for a very deep sense of relatedness to others. The negation, or forgetting of the self, "results in an opening of self to a sense of relatedness—intimate relatedness—with a greater whole, whether it be that of people in love or that of family, group, nation, or even some sense of cosmic consciousness. In any case, what arises is quite a different sense of self, that of the self as expanded and in a considerably wider relationship."[29]

As Watsuji sees it, being human as *ningen* is not a matter of belonging to a community at the expense of one's identity or being an individual at the expense of forging meaningful bonds with others. Rather, concrete human existence, Watsuji argues, is neither an individualistic experience *nor* an experience of being completely dissolved into society; rather, "*ningen* is the public and, at the same time, the individual human beings living within it."[30] If one reads Watsuji carefully, it is clear that, while the concept of relationality is certainly foregrounded in looking at ethics, *neither* one of these dimensions of human being-in-the-world, the individual or the social, is privileged in his theory of *ningen*. As he says: "*Ningen* denotes the unity of these contradictories. Unless we keep this dialectical structure in mind, we cannot understand the essence of *ningen*."[31] And the "unity" is not to be confused with something static, for it is always dialectical. This will be important to our understanding of Irigaray on female subjectivity in chapter 5. As Watsuji explains, through the movement of negation, human being as *ningen* involves a "transformation from being to nothingness, and from nothingness to being,"[32] *yet without eliminating all differentiation*: "the double negation . . . is not a complete negation that obliterates that which is negated. The identity of self-contradiction makes clear that that which is negated *is preserved*, else there would be no self-contradiction."[33] So again, we see that the negation inherent in Watsuji's concept of *ningen* is not something nihilistic.

This notion of negation and self-contradiction challenges patterns of dualistic thinking—of either/or logic. One is, as *ningen*, rather, both . . . and . . . :

> For human beings it is not that the individual and the whole are something fixed that necessarily exclude each other. Rather, an individual is an individual only when in a whole, and the whole is a whole only in individuals. When the whole is considered, the conflicts among many individuals must be recognized; and when individuals are spoken of, the unifying whole must be understood to be that which underlies all of them. In other words, an individual is an individual in its connection with multiplicity and individuality. Human beings possess this dynamic structure of reciprocal transformation.[34]

In *Climate and Culture*, Watsuji explains that by "human being" he means:

> not the individual (*anthropos, homo, homme*, etc.) but man both in this individual sense and at the same time man in society, the combination of the association of man. This duality is the essential nature of man. . . . For a true and full understanding, one must treat man both as individual and as whole.[35]

Even though Watsuji here uses the term "duality," in characterizing the self as individual and social, what is key for our reading of Watsuji is to pay close attention to the use, in the last sentence, of the "both . . . and . . ." structure. The "duality" as should be clear now, is *not* a matter of mutual exclusion or opposition, rather of dynamic tension, or an inclusive duality—what I call *nondualism* throughout the book. This is not a duality that divides or excludes; rather it is one that can be inclusive or dynamic. This concept reaches its fullest development in *Ethics*, where we see that Watsuji's theory of *ningen* reflects

> a dialectical unity of those double characteristics that are inherent in a human being. In so far as it is a human being, *ningen* as an individual differs completely from society. Because it does not refer to society, it must refer to individuals alone. Hence an individual is never communal with other individuals. Oneself and others are absolutely separate. Nevertheless, insofar as *ningen* also refers to the public, it is also through and through that community which exists between person and person, thus signifying society as well, and not just isolated human beings. Precisely because of its not being human beings in isolation, it is *ningen*. Hence, oneself and the other are absolutely separated from each other but, nevertheless, become one in communal existence. Individuals are basically different from society and yet dissolve themselves into society. *Ningen* denotes the unity of these contradictories.[36]

The relational aspect of human being-in-the-world is implicit then from the beginning in Watsuji's description of *ningen*. Indeed, this lack was one of Watsuji's initial problems with Heidegger's work. He states that Heidegger "treated human existence as being the existence of a man. From the standpoint of the dual structure both—individual and social—of human existence, he did not advance beyond an abstraction of a single aspect."[37] Contrasting Heidegger's idea of the being-with of Da-sein with Watsuji's *ningen* will bring his criticism into focus.

Heidegger: "The Solitary Self"

While Heidegger in his later work moved toward a recognition of the importance of relations for the self, toward a more complete concept of being-with, his concept of self still remained largely individual.[38] Despite the fact that Heidegger maintained that along with the primordiality of Da-sein's being-in-the-world, Da-sein is also always already being-with[39] and that being-with "existentially determines Da-sein even when another is not factically present and perceived,"[40] he does not explain being-with in any satisfactory manner. We are given at most, a descriptive phenomenological analysis. Interestingly, one of Heidegger's criticisms of Kant's concept of the self as subject, is that, as for Descartes, "the I again was forced back to an *isolated* subject that accompanies representations."[41] However, as Christopher Fynsk points out, despite Heidegger's break with the tradition of positing an isolated subject as the starting point of an investigation into human being-in-the-world, "his analysis of Da-sein in *Being and Time* leads back insistently to the solitary self."[42] Despite the fact that Heidegger states that "the understanding of others already lies in the understanding of being of Da-sein because its being is being-with,"[43] for the most part Da-sein is not in the world in such a way that it recognizes this understanding of others.

In everyday being-in-the-world Da-sein is subsumed in the world of the "they"; Da-sein is not itself; rather in the they, in its being with others, Da-sein's authentic self disappears:

> This being-with-one-another dissolves one's own Da-sein completely into the kind of being of 'the others' in such a way that the others, as distinguishable and explicitly, disappear more and more. In this inconspicuousness and unascertainability, the they unfolds its true dictatorship. We enjoy ourselves and have fun the way *they* enjoy themselves. We read, see, and judge literature and art the way *they* see and judge. But we also withdraw from the 'great mass' the way *they* withdraw, we find 'shocking' what *they* find shocking. The they, which is nothing definite and which all are, though not as a sum, prescribes the kind of being of everydayness.[44]

In the everyday being-in-the-world the true nature of being-with is masked, for Da-sein has lost itself in the they, where there is no differentiation from one Da-sein to the next, for "[e]veryone is the other, and no one is himself."[45] We can already see how different this is from the notion of being-with inherent in *ningen*. Whereas for Watsuji being-with-others is part of the true nature of *ningen*, for Heidegger, being-with-others in the they hides the true nature of Da-sein—its individuality.

In his discussion of authenticity, Heidegger stresses Da-sein's primordial being-in-the-world just as much as he did in the analysis of inauthentic Da-sein: "As *authentic being-a-self*, resoluteness does not detach Da-sein from its world, nor does it isolate it as free floating ego. How could it, if resoluteness as authentic disclosedness is, after all, nothing other than *authentically being-in-the-world?*"[46] So we get the sense that Da-sein *is* firmly in the world, but the problem is that Heidegger's insistence on the solitariness of authentic Da-sein makes it difficult to understand how authentic being-with plays out.

In the world then, Da-sein is mostly its inauthentic self, subsumed by the they and not genuinely being-with others. In fact, Heidegger states that "*Initially*, 'I' 'am' not in the sense of my own self, but I am the others in the mode of the they. In terms of the they, and as the they, I am initially 'given' to 'myself.' Initially, Da-sein is the they and for the most part it remains so."[47] This is inauthentic being-oneself and inauthentic being-with-others. Recall, however, that Heidegger wants to maintain that primordially, as authentic, Da-sein *does* genuinely understand others. Only as authentic, then, can this being-with be genuine, originary and radical. The problem in understanding what authentic being-with-others means arises due to the stress Heidegger places on the solitary nature of authentic Da-sein.

Authenticity as authentic being-toward-death remains for the most part utterly *non-relational* and Da-sein's *ownmost* possibility, and clearly a concept grounded in the temporal rather than the spatial:

> Being toward it discloses to Da-sein its *ownmost* potentiality-of-being in which it is concerned about the being of Da-sein absolutely. Here the fact can become evident to Da-sein that in the eminent possibility of itself it is torn away from the they, that is, anticipation can always already have torn itself away from the they.[48]

This must introduce a new kind of being-with, for being-with up to this point has been in the everydayness of Da-sein's being-in-the-world, in its submersion in the they, which has hindered Da-sein's being authentic. As Heidegger states:

> The nonrelational character of death understood in anticipation individualizes Da-sein down to itself. . . . It reveals the fact that any being-together-with what is taken care of and any being-with the others fails when one's ownmost potentiality-of-being is at stake. Da-sein can *authentically* be *itself* only when it makes that possible of its own accord.[49]

It seems as if *any* kind of being-with would be incompatible with authentic Da-sein, because, in authentic anticipation of being-toward-death Da-sein must be individualized down to itself only. Indeed, Heidegger's own insistence on the non-relational aspect of authenticity leads us to this conclusion. This is the paradoxical position which led Christopher Fynsk to claim that there is a continual return of Heidegger's analysis of Da-sein to a solitary self. Michael Theunissen phrases the paradox in the following manner: "Since being-in-the-world becomes authentic together with the self, being with Others must also participate in authenticity. . . . The question is, however, how individualization and authentic communalization can be thought together *concretely*."[50]

True to form, Heidegger has radically reinterpreted a traditional philosophical concept. Being-with is something that would normally be construed as relational. But on Heidegger's interpretation, authentic relations between people become centered on individuation, on freeing oneself precisely from the others in order to recognize them as apart from oneself. For him, authentic being-with is, in fact, being alone, freeing the other from me: "Letting be, however, which from a positive standpoint stands for the recognition of the ownmost being of Others, is, from a negative standpoint, the dissolution of all direct connection between Others and me. Others can only be freed *for themselves* inasmuch as they are freed *from me*."[51] Da-sein was directly with others only in inauthenticity, in the world of the they; as authentic, Da-sein's being-with is indirect.[52] In fact, Da-sein "achieves its authentic self without the positive connection of *Dasein*-with."[53] It is this lack of positive connection with others that sits uneasily with us as part of a phenomenological analysis meant to elucidate our being-in-the-world, an aspect of which is being-with-others. Heidegger proposes a being-with with no concrete relational aspects. For Watsuji's concept of ethics as *ningengaku*, however, such a being-with is unacceptable. Heidegger's Da-sein finds authenticity as a primarily temporal being—a being-toward-death, a being that anticipates its death. There is no significant spatial aspect to Da-sein's authenticity—there is no *space* for being-with. Watsuji, however, in contrast and reaction to this lack of the spatial in Heidegger, which precludes authentic being-with, creates a space where "individualization" and "communalization" can, not only be thought, but lived together between the abstract poles of individual and community as *ningen*. Rather than simply rejecting Heidegger's concepts of authenticity and inauthenticity, though, he appropriates them by inverting them—locating the inauthentic precisely where Heidegger locates the authentic.

Viewed in the context of Watsuji's philosophical system, Heidegger's description of Da-sein was destined to be unsatisfying because it did not allow room for the social, for community, for concrete authentic being-with. Indeed, "to attempt to comprehend the individual and society as the double or dual characteristic of *ningen* and thereby to uncover there humankinds' most authentic essence, can by no means be implemented from a standpoint that presupposes a primary distinction between individual and society."[54] This was why, for Watsuji, no adequate ethics can come out of Heidegger's philosophy—Heidegger views relations from a point of view of the individual only. In Watsuji's system, this is a "misconception," and because his concept of *ningen* takes both elements of human being-in-the-world into account, any study of the human being must also be a study of ethics.

In his earlier work, *Climate and Culture*, Wastuji begins the development of *ningen* by appropriating Heideggerian concepts. He argues that by virtue of relegating spatiality to something dependent on temporality, Heidegger neglected a key aspect of selfhood—betweenness. Yet Watsuji does not eliminate temporality from his concept of self; in fact he agrees with the importance of the self's historicity. What he adds to Heidegger's account is the recognition that the self's temporality and spatiality are inextricably linked. While Heidegger came to recognize this only in his later work, Watsuji saw it immediately.

Once one admits the irreducible spatiality of human beings, the concept of self that arises could never be that of the purely individual consciousness which arose out of Heidegger's key error of ignoring this aspect of Da-sein. For as we saw, Da-sein, at its most authentic moment, in its being-toward-death, is fundamentally individuated and *must* be so to be truly authentic. Watsuji's critical appropriation of Heidegger is evident when, in elucidating the link between climate and history, space and time, he uses the very example used by Heidegger to demonstrate the primordiality of the temporal—death:

> Here also we see clearly the duality of human existence—the finite and the infinite. Men die; their world changes; but through this unending death and change, man lives and his world continues. It continues incessantly through ending incessantly. In the individual's eyes it is a case of an "existence for death," but from the standpoint of society it is an "existence for life."[55]

Watsuji's use of the expression "existence for death" is clearly an appropriation of Heidegger's "being-toward-death," which is temporal, a "non-relational possibility," "free of the illusions of the They."[56] Here, however, implicit in Watsuji's use of the expression, is the criticism that Heidegger missed the essential social element of both life *and* death. He adds the spatiality of the social, the between, to the concept and inverts it. We can also see intimations above of the movement of negation of *ningen* that he develops in *Ethics*—that even the ultimate dissolving of self—death—leads to continual becoming in the world. Watsuji, as we see in the concept of *ningen*, finds authenticity precisely where Heidegger found inauthenticity: in the world of "the they."

Another Heideggerian notion that Watsuji appropriates in the elucidation of his concept of climate is "tools." Consider the following passage:

> There is much to be learnt from the thought that such tools are to be found very near to hand in human life. A tool is essentially "for doing something." A hammer is for beating, a shoe for wearing. But the object that is "for doing something else" has an immanent connection with the purpose for which it is employed. The hammer, for example is a tool for making shoes, and shoes, again, are tools for walking. The essential character of the tool lies in its being "for a purpose," lies, that is, in this purpose-relation.[57]

Juxtapose the above passage with the following from *Being and Time*:[58]

> A useful thing is essentially "something in order to . . . ". The different kinds of "in order to" such as serviceability, helpfulness, usability, handiness, constitute a totality of useful things. The structure of "in order to" contains a *reference* of something to something. . . . As the *what-for* of the hammer, plane and needle, the work to be produced has in its turn the kind of being of a useful thing. The shoe to be produced is for wearing (footgear), the clock is made for telling time.[59]

There can be little doubt that Watsuji borrowed his notion of tools from Heidegger—and in this particular example there is no critical aspect to the appropriation. So, one might ask, what, if anything, is the difference between his concept and Heidegger's? The difference is that whereas Heidegger goes on to show, in *Being and Time*, that the creation and use of tools has its place in the *inauthentic* world of the "they," Watsuji shows in *Ethics* that it is precisely in the world of the "they," in our being-in-the-world with others, where *authenticity* is to be found. This is foreshadowed even in *Climate and Culture*. Immediately following the citation given above, Watsuji states that "this purpose-relation finds its final origin in climatic self-comprehension."[60] Rather than resulting in an immersion in a world where the self is lost, Watsuji demonstrates that tools, if we examine their origins, lead us to a place wherein the self is found. Watsuji is very aware of turning Heidegger's concepts upside down, and deliberately appropriates and inverts Heidegger's authentic/inauthentic vocabulary. There are hints of this in the example from *Climate and Culture* above, but in *Ethics* he does this openly. As Shigenori Nagatomo explains:

> In Watsuji's ethical scheme, where the betweenness of an 'I' and the other is held to be nondual through the mediation of emptiness, what Heidegger called 'authentic' turns out to be inauthentic. . . . Personal existence gains its status of existence only in opposition to the other, and as such it is the negation of the wholeness of the human being-in-betweenness. However, for Watsuji, living nondual betweenness is authentic, and personal existence returns to this ground of authenticity via self-negation. Heidegger's authenticity is inauthentic precisely because it deviates from nondual betweenness.[61]

In contrast then, with the importance of the space of betweenness in *ningen*, in Heidegger's Da-sein analysis, temporal, individual Da-sein is the focus. For Watsuji we see again, intrinsic spatiality and dynamism are inherent in the concept of *ningen*—the space of betweenness. This comes out in his comparison of the German term *Welt* (world) with the Japanese *yononaka* and *seken* (which can both be translated as "public"). He argues that, while the German term includes the significance of the world of nature and the notion of community, the Japanese terms have a "plus value" out of which an ethics almost naturally arises:

> the term *Welt* signifies a generation, or a 'group,' a sum total of people or the place where people live. But as time went on, it came to lose this spatio-temporal significance, and finally came to mean one-sidedly the world as the sum total of objective natural things. On the other hand, so far as *seken* or *yononaka* are concerned, the meaning of something subjectively extended, which undergoes constant transformation, has been tenaciously preserved. Hence, the concept of *seken* already involves the historical, climatic, and social structure of human existence.[62]

We see here the idea of being *in relationship with* the world in a constant mutual transformation with others rather than an objectifying of them. This echoes Kasulis's discussion of the concept of intimacy. This intimacy is a moving beyond the individual ego found in Heidegger and the West and "a recognition of the interdependent and dependent side of human existence."[63] It is the recognition of human being as *ningen* as the dynamic interrelation that is, if genuine, a human becoming as much as a human being.

While in *Ethics*, Watsuji cites only Husserl's "Phenomenology of Internal Time Consciousness," briefly analyzing *ningen* alongside Husserl's concept of intersubjectivity will further elucidate Watsuji's ethical theory of self and show how his concept of *ningen* can take us beyond even Husserl's intersubjectivity.

Husserl: Moving toward a Relational Self

It might seem that Edmund Husserl's concept of self has more in common with Wastuji's notion than Heidegger's. After all, he recognizes that from the outset, one is in an intersubjective world. However, on closer inspection, it is clear that he too rests his analysis on the intentionality of the *individual* consciousness.

From the outset, Husserl maintains the following:

> within myself, within the limits of my transcendentally reduced pure conscious life, I *experience* the world (including others)—and, according to its experiential sense, *not* as (so to speak) my *private* synthetic formation but as other than

mine alone [*mir fremde*], as an *intersubjective* world, actually there for everyone, accessible in respect of its Objects to everyone.[64]

Referring to Husserl's concept of self in *Ideas II*, James Drummond observes:

The individual, personal being, is constituted in those dependencies on intersubjective experiential life which involve communicative experience, for it is in those acts that the individual sets himself or herself off against those other subjects, all of whom together form a social association. Thus, we see that the personal and social are reciprocally co-constituted.[65]

In contradistinction to Heidegger's philosophy, Husserl does not think that the individual being is lost in its relation with others; rather, Husserl recognizes the interconnectedness of self and other and the world they create together. In the opening of section 55, of *Cartesian Meditations*, "Establishment of the Community of Monads. The First Form of Objectivity: Intersubjective Nature," Husserl states that "it is more important to clarify the *community*, developing at various levels, which is produced forthwith by virtue of experiencing someone else."[66] Contrary to Heidegger's notion of the inauthentic world of the they, Husserl's notion of community recognizes the deep interdependence between self and other and how this is constitutive of the formation of self. He goes on to state:

The first thing constituted in the form of community, and the *foundation for all other intersubjectively common things*, is the *commonness of Nature*, along with that of the *Other's organism* and *his psychophysical Ego*, as paired with *my own psychophysical Ego*.[67]

It is clear then, that Husserl's concept of community is both defined by and defining for a concept of self. In *Ideas II*, he tells us that the surrounding world

is comprised not only of individual persons, but the persons are instead members of communities, members of personal unities of a higher order, which, as totalities, have their own lives, preserve themselves by lasting through time despite the joining or leaving of individuals, have their qualities as communities. . . . The members of the community, of marriage and of the family, of the social class, of the union, of the borough, of the state, of the church, etc., "know" themselves as their members, consciously realize that they are dependent on them, and perhaps consciously react back on them.[68]

Husserl's idea of being-there-for-others is reflected in his concept of community and is much richer than what we found in Heidegger, and evocative, at first glance anyway, of Watsuji. As the last sentence of this passage shows, a community, for Husserl, be it family, marriage, state, etc., has a hand in defining the self.

For Husserl, the community cannot exist without the participation of the person.[69] But it is not clear that the inverse holds—that the person cannot exist without the community. Turning to section 56 of *Cartesian Meditations*, "Constitution of Higher Levels of Intermonadic Community," we do see that the "first and lowest" level of community, between myself and others is not, as Husserl puts it, "just nothing." He states:

> Whereas, really inherently, each monad is an absolutely separate unity, the 'irreal' intentional reaching of the other into my primordiality is not irreal in the sense of being dreamt into it or being present to consciousness after the fashion of a mere phantasy. *Something that exists is in intentional communion with something else that exists.* It is an essentially *unique connectedness*, an actual community and precisely the one that makes transcendentally possible the being of a world, a world of men and things.[70]

It is this unique connectedness of individuals that makes possible the community, the world in which individuals themselves develop. The relationship between individuals and community is *co*-constituting. Husserl maintains that even when conceived of as an individual, solitary human being, the sense "member of a community" belongs to her—"there is implicit a *mutual being for one another*."[71]

According to Husserl, I constitute the community and the other within myself, and in turn I am constituted within the other who also constitutes the community with me.[72] Self and other meet together in the space of community, "where men and each particular man are vitally immersed in a concrete surrounding world, are related to it in undergoing and doing. . . . With this continual change in the human life-world, manifestly *the men themselves also change as persons*, since correlatively they must always be taking on new habitual properties."[73] We hear a resonance here with Watsuji's *ningen* and its process of mutual transformation in the betweenness that is concrete ethical being-in-the-world.

Still, Watsuji thinks that Husserl's position does not go far enough in recognizing the interdependence of the self and the social. He maintains that it is not that we should look to man *and* his relationships, or the human being *in* her relationships, but that "betweenness" (*aidagara*) is a constitutive part of what human being is and to ignore this is to misunderstand human being at a fundamental level. Betweenness, or *aidagara*, according to Watsuji, implies "a living and dynamic betweenness, as a subjective interconnection of acts."[74] Betweenness is both a part of the individual and a part of the social and is reinforced every time we act: "We cannot sustain ourselves in any *aida* [between] . . . without acting subjectively. At the same time, we cannot act without maintaining ourselves in some *aida*."[75]

The similarity with Husserl then, only goes so far and there is an important difference to pay attention to. First of all, Husserl states that "really inherently, each monad is an absolutely separate unity," indicating, that for him, one is essentially an individual. This, in fact, is an example of Kasulis's integrity model of self and its primacy on external relations, where, although "I find myself connected to many other things, none of these things is literally part of me."[76] Furthermore, as Watsuji points out, his concept of *ningen* differs from that of Husserl in that, for him:

> *Betweenness* is quite distinct from the intentionality of consciousness. Activity inherent in the consciousness of an 'I' is never determined by this 'I' alone but is also determined by others. It is not merely a reciprocal activity in that oneway conscious activities are performed one after another, but, rather, that either one of them is at once determined by both sides; that is, by itself and by the other. Hence, so far as betweenness-oriented existences are concerned, each consciousness interpenetrates the other.[77]

Watsuji's notion of interpenetration of consciousnesses, which speaks to the permeability of self and other—the fundamental emptiness of their distinction—goes beyond Husserl's intersubjectivity, which always has the starting point of *my* consciousness. In betweenness, there is no one consciousness that has priority (recall Lafleur's explanation of the individual and social being "coequal" from the outset), precisely because it is a nondualistic concept that does not fit into a binary framework in which one side or the other is given priority.

Watsuji's betweenness adds a further element of connection with the other to Husserl's intersubjectivity, which still rests firmly on the idea of an isolated ego, recognizing that not only do I *liken* my psychic life to that of the other, but that the psychic life of the other *penetrates* mine and vice versa: "When *Thou* gets angry, my consciousness may be entirely coloured by Thou's expressed anger, and when I feel sorrow, Thou's consciousness is influenced by I's sorrow. It can never be argued that consciousness of such a self is independent,"[78] in terms of being an independent ego as we have seen through our discussion of the movement of negation inherent in *ningen*. Watsuji further argues that this I/Thou interpenetration of consciousnesses occurs not only in intimate relationships with friends or family, but even in temporary relationships in the community—when riding the bus for example[79]—for even there, I, the individual, am also at the same time a member of the community of those riding the bus with me.

In this chapter we have seen what Watsuji finds unsatisfying in both Heidegger's and Husserl's analyses of self with respect to the spatial or relational aspect. We have seen how neither Heidegger's nor Husserl's views of self, on Watsuji's analysis, express the fullness of what it is to be an ethical human being-in-the-world. Another aspect of the spatial self that Watsuji finds lacking certainly in Heidegger, but also ultimately in Husserl, is the body. In chapter 3 we will turn to a detailed examination of the body and its role in the constitution of a concept of self and ethics.

Notes

1. For more on Watsuji's life see Robert E. Carter, "Introduction to Watsuji Tetsurō's Rinrigaku" in Wastuji Tetsurō's Rinrigaku: Ethics in Japan, trans. Yamamoto Seisaku and Robert E. Carter (Albany: SUNY Press, 1996), 1–6, Robert E. Carter "Watsuji Tetsurō," in the Stanford Internet Encylcopedia of Philosophy, http://plato .stanford.edu/entries/watsuji-Tetsurō/#Bib, and David Dilworth, Valdo H. Viglielmo with Agustin Jacinto Zavala, "Chapter Four: Watsuji Tetsurō," in Sourcebook for Modern Japanese Philosophy (Westport: Greenwood Press, 1998), 221–225.

2. Watsuji Tetsurō, Climate and Culture, trans. Geoffrey Bownas (New York: Greenwood Press, Inc. in cooperation with Yushodo Co., Ltd., 1988), v.

3. For more detailed studies of Watsuji and Heidegger see Erin McCarthy, The Spatiality of the Self (Ph.D. dissertation, University of Ottawa, 2000) and Graham Mayeda, Time, Space and Ethics in the Philosophy of Watsuji Tetsurō, Kuki Shuzo and Martin Heidegger (New York: Routledge, 2006).

4. Watsuji Tetsurō, Wastuji Tetsurō's Rinrigaku: Ethics in Japan, trans. Yamamoto Seisaku and Robert E. Carter (Albany: SUNY Press, 1996), 9. (Hereafter referred to as Ethics).

5. Watsuji, Ethics, 10.

6. Watsuji, Ethics, 15.

7. John Maraldo, "Watsuji Tetsurō's Ethics: Totalitarian or Communitarian?" in Komparative Ethik: Das gute Leben zwischen den Kulturen, ed. Rolf Elberfeld and Günter Wohlfart (Köln: edition chōra, 2002), 185.

8. Maraldo, "Watsuji Tetsurō's Ethics," 185.

9. Watsuji, Ethics, 19.

10. Watsuji, Ethics, 19.

11. Kasulis, Intimacy, 61.

12. William R. Lafleur, "Buddhist Emptiness in Watsuji Tetsurō," Religious Studies 14 (1978): 243. My emphasis.

13. See LaFleur, "Buddhist Emptiness."

14. See Watsuji, Ethics, chapter 6.

15. Watsuji, Ethics, 117.

16. LaFleur, "Buddhist Emptiness," 244.

17. Robert E. Carter, "Interpretive Essay: Strands of Influence," in Watsuji *Tetsurō's Rinrigaku: Ethics in Japan*. Trans. Yamamoto Seisaku and Robert E. Carter, 350. Albany: SUNY Press, 1996.

18. Kasulis, *Intimacy*, 58.

19. Watsuji, *Ethics*, 117.

20. Watsuji, *Ethics*, 117.

21. Watsuji, *Ethics*, 101.

22. Isamu Nagami, "The Ontological Foundation in Tetsurō Watsuji's Philosophy: *Kū* and Human Existence" *Philosophy East and West* 31.3 (July 1981): 283–284.

23. Kasulis, *Zen Action/Zen Person* (Honolulu: University of Hawaii Press, 1981), 24.

24. Carter, "Strands of Influence," 332.

25. Watsuji, *Ethics*, 99.

26. Carter, "Strands of Influence," 332.

27. Watsuji, *Ethics*, 117–118.

28. Carter, "Strands of Influence," 340.

29. Carter, "Strands of Influence," 334.

30. Watsuji, *Ethics*, 15.

31. Watsuji, *Ethics*, 15.

32. Watsuji, *Ethics*, 19.

33. Carter, "Strands of Influence," 341.

34. Watsuji, *Ethics*, 124.

35. Watsuji, *Climate*, 8–9.

36. Watsuji, *Ethics*, 15.

37. Watsuji, *Climate*, v–vi.

38. See, for example, "Building Dwelling Thinking," trans. Albert Hofstadter, in *Poetry, Language, Thought* (New York: Harper and Row, 1971), 143–162. See also Erin McCarthy, *The Spatiality of the Self*.

39. Martin Heidegger, *Being and Time*, trans. Joan Stambaugh (Albany: State University of New York Press, 1996. Trans. of *Sein und Zeit*. 17th ed. Tübingen: Max Niemeyer Verlag, 1993), 107/114.

40. Heidegger, *Being and Time*, 113/120.

41. Heidegger, *Being and Time*, 295–296/321.

42. Christopher Fynsk, *Heidegger: Thought and Historicity*, (Ithaca: Cornell University Press, 1986), 28.

43. Heidegger, *Being and Time*, 116/123.

44. Heidegger, *Being and Time*, 119/127.

45. Heidegger, *Being and Time*, 120/128.

46. Heidegger, *Being and Time*, 274/298.

47. Heidegger, *Being and Time*, 121/129.

48. Heidegger, *Being and Time*, 243/263.

49. Heidegger, *Being and Time*, 243/263.

50. Michael Theunissen, *The Other: Studies in the Social Ontology of Husserl, Heidegger, Sartre, and Buber*, trans. Christopher Macann (Cambridge, Mass.: The MIT Press, 1984), 189.

51. Theunissen, *The Other*, 191.

52. Theunissen, *The Other*, 189–190.

53. Theunissen, *The Other*, 192 n. 34.

54. Watsuji, *Ethics*, 14.

55. Watsuji, *Climate*, 9–10.

56. Heidegger, *Being and Time*, 244/264, 245/266.

57. Watsuji, *Climate*, 13.

58. Note that Joan Stambaugh translates *Zeug* as "'useful thing" in her translation of *Being and Time*, which I use here (Albany: SUNY Press, 1996).

59. Heidegger, *Being and Time*, 64/68–65/70.

60. Watsuji, *Climate*, 13.

61. Shigenori Nagatamo, review of "Watsuji Tetsurō, *Watsuji Tetsurō's Rinrigaku: Ethics in Japan*," *The Eastern Buddhist*, 30.1 (1997): 156.

62. Watsuji, *Ethics*, 18–19

63. Thomas P. Kasulis, "Intimacy: A General Orientation in Japanese Religious Values," *Philosophy East and West* 40.4 (October 1990): 448.

64. Edmund Husserl, *Cartesian Meditations*, trans. Dorion Cairns. (The Hague: Martinus Nijhoff, 1967. Trans. of *Cartesianische Meditationen und Pariser Vorträge. Husserliana*, vol. 1, 2nd ed. Ed. S. Strasser. The Hague: Martinus Nijhoff, 1973), 91.

65. James Drummond, "The 'Spiritual World: The Personal, the Social and the Communal," in *Issues in Husserl's Ideas II* (Dordrecht: Kluwer, 1996), 243.

66. Husserl, *Cartesian*, 120.

67. Husserl, *Cartesian*, 120.

68. Husserl, *Ideas Pertaining to a Pure Phenomenology and to a Phenomenological Philosophy: Second Book: Studies in the Phenomenology of Constitution*, trans. R. Rojcewicz and A. Schuwer (Dordrecht: Kluwer, 1989), 192.

69. See Drummond, "Spiritual World," 238.

70. Husserl, *Cartesian*, 129.

71. Husserl, *Cartesian*, 129.

72. See Husserl, *Cartesian*, 130.

73. Husserl, *Cartesian*, 135.

74. Watsuji, *Ethics*, 18.

75. Watsuji, *Ethics*, 18.

76. Kasulis, *Intimacy*, 61.

77. Watsuji, *Ethics*, 69.

78. Watsuji, *Ethics*, 69.

79. Watsuji, *Ethics*, 70.

CHAPTER THREE

The Embodied Self

In the last chapter I argued that on Watsuji's view, both Heidegger's and Husserl's concepts of self and intersubjectivity fall short of giving a full account of human being-in-the-world, particularly with respect to the relational aspect of selfhood. For Watsuji, not only is self as *ningen* relational, but it is also embodied. On Watsuji's view, even Husserl, who includes the body in his phenomenology, fails to consider the body a truly integrated aspect of self. In this chapter, I first look at why Husserl's account of body isn't satisfying for Watsuji. I then explain that the fact that he falls short on Watsuji's view is not surprising in light of Japanese and feminist critiques of the way the body has been treated in Western philosophy more generally. Finally, I draw on both Japanese philosophy in general and Watsuji's philosophy in particular to provide a positive account of an embodied, ethical self, one that avoids these critiques.

Husserl and the Body

As noted, for Watsuji, *ningen*, as a betweenness-oriented being, encompasses the social, individual *and* embodied aspects of self. He states: "Insofar as betweenness is constituted, one human body is connected with another."[1] At first glance this seems not very different from Husserl's description of intersubjectivity. As he explains, our experience of the other "as appearing in my primordial sphere, is first of all a body in my primordial Nature."[2] More than for Heidegger, for whom the body only ever appears as fragments and not ever as a whole, lived body, Husserl, at least in some respects, sees the limits of Cartesian body-mind dualism and tries to overcome them. He seems to agree with Watsuji in recognizing that the separation of body and mind can only make sense if it is part of a phenomenological *abstraction*. He writes, for example:

> Men and animals have their position in space and move in space as sheer physical things. It will be said that it is obvious that they do so "by virtue of" their corporeal Bodies. It would be bizarre, however, to say that only the man's Body moved but not the man, that the man's Body walked down the street, drove in a car, dwelled in the country or town, but not the man.[3]

Husserl's description of how it would be odd *not* to recognize the integration of self and body seems convincing and commonsensical, yet he still views body as some "thing" that is possessed by the self, even as odd as it would be to describe it this way. To see this, consider, for example, Richard Zaner's description of the role of the body in Husserl's phenomenology as found in *Ideas I*. He writes:

> Consciousness can become "worldly" only by being embodied within the world as part of it. In so far as the world is material Nature, consciousness must partake of the transcendence of material Nature. That is to say, its transcendence is manifestly an embodiment in a material, corporeal body. Consciousness, thus, takes on the characteristic of being "here and now" (ecceity) by means of experiential (or, more accurately, its intentive) relation to that corporeal being which embodies it.[4]

If this were a nondualistic view, there would be no need to talk of a "relation" between consciousness and corporeal being, for on a nondualistic view they would be thought of as one from the outset. Here, the body still seems to be acting as a container for consciousness, something inhabited by the self or imbued with it. The passage, then, still reflects dualist assumptions and it is clear that, for Husserl, "we experience the world itself dualistically . . . as a collection of discrete objects . . . causally interacting in space and time."[5] This is not to deny that Husserl at least puts dualism into question:

> People and animals *have* material Bodies, and to that degree they have spatiality and materiality. According to what is specifically human and animal, that is, according to what is psychic, they *are* however, not material, and, consequently, taken *also as concrete totalities*, they are *not material* realities in the proper sense. Material things are open to fragmentation, something which accompanies the extension that belongs to their essence. But men and animals

cannot be fragmented. Men and animals are *spatially localized;* and even what is psychic about them, at least in virtue of its essential foundedness in the Bodily, partakes of the spatial order.[6]

Here Husserl acknowledges that there is some kind of *essential* spatial element to the self and that this somehow extends to the psyche—he seems even to be reaching for a vocabulary or framework of nondualism. Nevertheless, despite the fact that he says consciousness needs the body in order to become worldly, that the body needs consciousness in order to move from being a mere physical body (*Körper*) to being an animate organism (*Leib*) and that even what is psychic about being human has some spatiality or grounding in the body, it is still clear that he conceives of the psychic as in some sense independent of the body.

The same tendency is seen in *Ideas II,* chapter 4, "The Constitution of Psychic Reality in Empathy." Here Husserl recognizes the role of the body in human relations. He says that while we identify another human being first by recognizing a body similar to ours, empathy is what allows us to complete that picture—to identify another as being like me:

In my physical surrounding world I encounter Bodies, i.e., material things of the same type as the material thing constituted in solipsistic experience, "my Body," and I apprehend them as Bodies, that is, I feel by empathy that in them there is an Ego-subject, along with everything that pertains to it and with the particular content demanded from case to case. Transferred over to the other Bodies thereby is first of all that "localization" I accomplish in various sense-fields (field of touch, warmth, coldness, smell, taste, pain, sensuous pleasure) and sense-regions (sensations of movement), and then in a similar way there is a transfer of my indirect localization of spiritual activities.[7]

On his account, empathy allows us to see the other as *similar* to ourselves, and this occurs through the body and in space and time. He even acknowledges that empathy is founded on a bodily relation with the other:

In order to establish a mutual relationship between myself and an other, in order to communicate something to him, a Bodily relation, a Bodily connection by means of physical occurrences, must be instituted. I have to go over and speak to him.[8]

Nevertheless, for all of Husserl's talk of the selves as conscious beings in bodies, he still sees a separation between self and other and thus his concept of empathy falls short of the sort of interpenetration of consciousness of which Watsuji speaks. Husserl recognizes that in encounters with another human being, part of what we understand about her *and* ourselves comes by way of the body of the other—but this contribution to understanding does not go beyond the physical appearance of the other person. Nor does Husserl recognize a sense of connection with the other body, which, we have seen, is key for Watsuji. On his view, we transfer the physical aspects of ourselves to the understanding of the other and vice versa—understanding them on analogy with ourselves rather than by connecting with them. He says we recognize that not only does this other person have a body like mine, but "there also belongs . . . the interiority of psychic acts. In this connection it should be noted that the point of departure is here, too, a transferred co-presence: to the seen Body there belongs a psychic life, just as there does to my Body."[9] We see the holdover from Descartes here in Husserl's concept of the "interiority of psychic acts"—the mind is behind the scenes as it were—inside in a way we can't get at directly. Furthermore we see that these bodies and their minds remain fundamentally separated from each other—we can *liken* the other to ourselves, but we both remain locked in our own subjectivity. For Watsuji, this falls far short of true betweenness.

Husserl's problems in articulating anything beyond the dualistic, stem, perhaps, from the fact that he is operating from an integrity-based perspective, which, as we saw in chapter 1, makes a sharp divide between the intellectual and the somatic. Turning to an examination of the matter from an intimacy perspective—more specifically, to the views promoted by Japanese and feminist philosophy—we will better see the limits of this sort of divide.

Body East and West

In most of Western philosophy, the body has not, historically, been considered a site for knowledge, if it has been considered at all. As far back as Plato, the body was seen as something that is inimical to knowledge. In the *Republic*, for example, we learn that we must control the body with the mind—keep it in check lest it overtake us. Elizabeth Spelman notes: "According to Plato, the body, with its deceptive senses, keeps us from real knowledge; it rivets us in a world of material things which is far removed from the world of reality; and it tempts us away from the virtuous life."[10] The soul is that which attains knowledge, not the body. Self too, is situated in the soul, if not identified as soul, and the body is merely contingently related to it, or externally related, to use Kasulis's term.

The conception of the body modern philosophy inherited from Descartes shares this aspect of Plato's thought. For Descartes, the body is an inert object, animated and known by the mind but not something cognitive in itself. It is not a *knowing* body, rather a *known* body, an object among others in a mechanical world. As Drew Leder suggests in "A Tale of Two Bodies: The Cartesian Corpse and the Lived Body," seventeenth-century medicine is based "first and foremost, not upon the lived body, but upon the dead, or inanimate body."[11] The dead, inert body serves as a model for the living body. For Descartes the body is an automaton, moved by mechanical forces. For him, the "living body is not fundamentally different from the lifeless; it is a kind of animated corpse, a functioning mechanism."[12] It was not until the (relatively recent) advent of phenomenology and existentialism and then feminist philosophy that the concept of the lived body was given any philosophical importance in ethics and epistemology. In Japanese philosophy, however, a different picture of the body has long held sway. In this tradition, the body is viewed as necessary for knowledge, and there is an emphasis in much of Japanese philosophy on lived experience, in which the body is included as philosophically significant. Watsuji, for example, makes this point in his critique of the mind-body separation in Western philosophy. He states that "[w]hat is not in accord with the concrete facts of experience is the view that something psychological, accompanied by no bodily events, and a process of the physical body entirely unrelated to bodily experiences subsist in the form of an opposition between body and mind existing independent of each other."[13] For Watsuji, this opposition simply doesn't reflect our lived experience. In our everyday experience, we act as integrated embodied beings—we move through the day without having to resolve any conflict between our bodies and our minds, and we don't think of them as independent from each other. As David Shaner explains, in Japanese philosophy, particularly in Zen Buddhism, there is a very strong feeling of the interdependence of the mind and body—in fact, they are "inseparably connected" and as a result, "the body serves as a vehicle for, not a detriment to, the direct experience of . . . truth."[14] The term used in Japanese to express this view is "bodymind."[15]

The Western view of body as a hindrance or detriment to knowledge has then, for the most part, kept the body from being accorded a significant place in philosophy. As Elizabeth Grosz explains, the Western tradition associates man with the mind and woman with the body. Coupled with philosophy's view of itself as concerned with the mental—that is, the conceptual, the ideal, the theoretical, the abstract and the rational—as opposed to the body, which is viewed as practical, concrete, and non-rational, philosophy has "surreptitiously excluded femininity, and ultimately women, from its practices through its usually implicit coding of femininity with the unreason associated with the body."[16] Indeed Grosz goes so far as to state that since "the inception of philosophy as a separate and self-contained discipline in ancient Greece, philosophy has established itself on the foundations of a profound somatophobia."[17] What we end up with in most of the history of philosophy in the West, then, is a dichotomy of male/female being attached to the homologous hierarchical dichotomies of mind/body, reason/emotion, and so on. In these dichotomies, each side is set up in opposition to the other and the second term in the pair is always devalued.[18] We are left with a logic of either/or and there is no room for one of both-and that would allow each "side" to be valued. In Japanese philosophy, this is not the case for the mind/body pair, nor, even necessarily for male/female. This can be most clearly seen in the above-mentioned Buddhist concept of bodymind. From the nondualist perspective of bodymind, "mind is not necessarily higher than body." To the contrary, from this perspective "all diverse phenomena are identical as to their constituents within; all are in the state of constant transformation; no absolute difference exists between man and nature; body and mind are non-dual."[19] In other words, they work integrally and any thought of them as separate, hierarchical or oppositional is a false abstraction. The Japanese philosopher Yuasa Yasuo, one of Watsuji's last students, recognizes this historical lack of both body *and* the feminine in Western thought. Referring to the Daoist notion of body in his discussion of bodymind, the cultivation of *ki* energy and the importance of the balance of *yin-yang* in Chinese philosophy, Yuasa notes that in this system, "femininity and masculinity do not signify a *physiological* distinction between man and woman." As he then goes on to explain,

> To put it from a depth psychological point-of-view, a mature, all-round personality cannot be formed unless the power of femininity, rooted in the unconscious, complements the masculine tendency that surfaces in consciousness. When seen from this vantage point, the history of modern thought and philosophy initiated in the West discloses a situation, we might say, in which the power of masculinity has been a solo runner, fortifying rationalism as well as promoting the opposition and competition between "I" and "other," while the power of femininity has failed to function.[20]

So for Yuasa, in a certain sense, even the male/female dichotomy is false when taken as absolute.

In her analysis of Greek philosophy, Grosz notes how far back this emphasis on rationality and the mind goes: "In his doctrine of the Forms, Plato sees matter itself as a denigrated and imperfect version of the Idea. The body is a betrayal of and a prison for the soul, reason, or mind. For Plato, it was evident that reason should rule over the body and over the irrational or appetitive functions of the soul." Woman, as we saw earlier, was associated with the body and hence, "the binarization of the sexes, the dichotomization of the world and of knowledge has been effected already at the threshold of Western reason."[21] In Japanese philosophy we find an alternative model. Rather than being ignored or devalued, as is evident through the very term "bodymind," the two work together and in fact their integration must be cultivated rather than fled from or avoided. Zen master Dōgen, for example, "says that 'learning through the mind' must be united with 'learning through the body' (shinjitsunintai . . . 'truth' + 'reality' + 'human body,' literally 'the real human body')."[22] Regarding the difference between Eastern and Western philosophy, Yuasa states that that the "most fundamental difference is that the cultivation method does not accept the mind-body dichotomy that Descartes elevated to the status of a principle."[23]

Ningen, Ethics and the Body[24]

Watsuji's ethics defies Descartes' principle. While Husserl, as we saw, struggled to avoid the dualism associated with the mind-body problem, he was never able to completely overcome it. Regarding mind-body dualism, Watsuji states that "the crux of the problem becomes the realization that body is not mere matter; in other words, it is the problem of the self-active nature of the body."[25] He goes on to state that the self-active nature of the body has as its foundation the spatial and temporal structure of human life; "a self-active body cannot remain in isolation for its structure is dynamic, uniting in isolation and isolated within union."[26] This self-active body is, in fact, bodymind—here we see that the body is something active in itself, not a container or mere matter. We also note that Watsuji's characterization of bodymind here reflects ningen's movement of negation.

On this view, body is from the beginning an epistemological site for Watsuji—an essential element in attaining knowledge and identity—one that cannot be separated from self as ningen. Rather than limit knowledge, the body is an intimate part of the self's way of knowing. As Yuasa observes, "Watsuji's concept of betweenness, the subjective interconnection of meanings, must be grasped as a carnal interconnection. Moreover, this interconnection must not be thought of as either a psychological or physical relatedness, nor even their conjunction."[27] If this is hard to grasp, it is because Watsuji's understanding of the body goes beyond either/or binary frameworks to which we in the West are heirs. He challenges us to think differently about the ways in which we think about corporeal boundaries, and to integrate the body into ethics and the conception of human being.

Watsuji illustrates the concept of a knowing body, the oneness of body-mind, in two helpful examples. The first example he uses to express between-ness as bodily knowledge is the example of mother and child. In *Ethics* he writes:

> So far as physiological bodies are concerned, they can be spoken of as easily as individual trees. But this is not the case with bodies viewed as expressions of the subjective or as persons in their concrete qualities. A mother and her baby can never be conceived of as merely two independent individuals. A baby wishes for its mother's body, and the mother offers her breast to the baby. If they are separated from each other, both look for each other with all the more intensity. Since ancient times in Japan, any attempt to isolate two bodies such as these from each other has been described by the aphorism "to wrench green wood." As is evident, a mother's body and her baby's are somehow connected as though one. . . . This power of attraction, even though not physical attraction alone, is yet a real attraction connecting the two as though one.[28]

Mother and child know one another *bodily*, not just psychologically and their intimate connection goes beyond physical proximity or physiological dependence. For Watsuji, this betweenness, by virtue of being a part of *ningen*, encompasses the individual *and* embodied aspects of self as well as the social. In betweenness, a new space of relationship, an ethical space, is founded. This is clearly illustrated in his second example, that of friendship. He writes: "That one wishes to visit a friend implies that she intends to draw near to the friend's body. If she does go to visit a friend who is at some distance by streetcar, then her body moves in the friend's direction, attracted by the power that draws them together."[29] Here we see both Watsuji's concept of intimacy and oneness of body-mind. For him, relationship between two people is not merely psychological, a meeting of two separate minds—it cannot be separated from the relation of their bodies. We know our friends, in other words, with our "whole" nondualistic selves. For Watsuji the movement of the body in the carrying out of an act, for example, does not involve merely "physical relations nor biological ones. Instead, it involves as well the relationship between one subject and another, as distinct from the relation between a person and a thing."[30] This is the place of betweenness, the place of ethics.[31] It is significantly deeper than Husserl's conceptualization of bodies that seemed to reflect each other's characteristics, but never actually connect with the other bodymind.

As Yuasa points out, in his analysis of Watsuji, the concept of *ningen* cannot but involve embodiment: "To exist in betweenness is to exist within the life-space. Furthermore, to exist in a spatial *basho* [place or field] means nothing other than to exist as a human being by virtue of one's body; I exist in my body, occupying the spatial *basho* of here and now: This is what it means for me to exist within the world."[32] As Watsuji says,

> The viewing of a human body only as a solid material object does not call into question the reality of the subjective human body, although it does focus on the objective one. As a consequence, what is dealt with is nothing more than either a relationship between a subjective ego and an objective human body or a relationship between an objective ego and an objective human body. From ancient times this viewpoint has made it impossible to have a correct understanding of the human body.[33]

It has been impossible because on Watsuji's view, most of Western philosophy has been stuck in dualisms that viewed body as merely a container for mind, or a mere material object—as something separate from mind and self. Watsuji tells us that

> the question to ask is whether in our daily life we actually deal with the body as an object of physiology. Is it true to say, when we meet a friend and exchange greetings, that we take for granted that the greeting of our partner is a movement of our physiological body? Is it true to say, on seeing my friend run toward me while calling my name, that I pay attention only to such things as the vehement movement of muscle and the vibration of vocal chords? Everyone knows that this is not the case. In the movements of the human body, that is, in its behavior, we catch a glimpse of the expression of an acting subject, rather than the mere object of physiology.[34]

In other words, Watsuji expresses here the idea of embodied subjectivity wherein we see that the body's action is not merely the outer manifestation of an inner subjectivity. To think this is to make the same error all over again. Rather, the subject is embodied and so is the person with whom it is related. We see the other as bodymind right from the start and react from our positions as acting, embodied subjects as well.

While Yuasa points out that there is no explicit account of the body in Watsuji's work, it is clear that it nonetheless permeates his concept of *ningen* and is central to some of his most evocative examples of betweenness in ethics, which is, after all, "concerned with those problems that prevail between persons."[35] Watsuji does not believe that as betweenness-oriented beings that we have to have either only a mental connection between people or only a physical connection. Rather, such "connections are neither merely physical nor merely psychological or physical/psychological."[36] Such connections go beyond either/or binaries. For him, body is a site for knowledge and for ethics, involving not just the mind, not just the body, but both as intimately interconnected and interdependent: "When we are aware of something in our mind, this experience already involves the human body as an element within it."[37] In other words, we know not just with our minds, but also with our bodies. Watsuji gives the simple example of smiling with pleasure: "Within the bodily experience of pleasure a human body is already involved as a feeling and moving agent, which produces a smile, which is itself a bodily motion. Hence, this bodily motion is already filled with mind, which jumps with joy. The phrase 'a mind jumps with joy' already indicates the inseparability of mind and body."[38] Again, the smile is *not* simply a manifestation of a subjective state operating behind the scenes. The smile *is* the subjective state embodied—where no clear cut distinction between the mental and the physical can be made.

Watsuji believes that we have to work at seeing the body of another as a mere object—that a surgeon, for example, needs to work to develop such an attitude to be able to perform surgery well. Indeed, we know that soldiers are conditioned in practices of disembodiment.[39] They are trained to see other human beings as less than human, as not like me, as targets, as objects, rather than subjective human beings. To create such abstractions, we have to *think* our way to them; we must rationalize them and find methods through which to keep the body separate from the mind whether in our own life experience, or in dealing with others in betweenness. This is not only the case for someone like a soldier who is faced with killing another human being, but consider also the case of a victim of abuse, whose only recourse in the midst of suffering physical abuse may be to attempt to dissociate herself from her body. What both examples show is that such abstractions are exceptions and most often are contrary to our lived, embodied experience of the world.

A further example illustrates the fact that it is contrary to everyday being-in-the-world to treat a human being *either* as a *mere* physical solid or as a *mere* psychic entity:

When I discover a friend of mine waiting for me beside a bronze statue, the friend is never immediately given merely as a material solid having the same form as the statue. Instead, I discover my friend there, from the beginning. When I shake hands with my friend it is not that I first touch her hand as a material solid and afterwards come to infer that this material solid is put into motion by my friend's mind. Rather, from the outset, I touch my friend herself. There is no momentary period of time in which a human body is experienced as a mere material solid.[40]

As long as the human body plays a role in this betweenness, which it must, due to its self-active nature, the fact that it is not mere matter—we cannot, according to Watsuji, ever treat it or view it as a mere material solid, as mere machine. We must treat it as part of the betweenness of human beings, the place of ethics.

For Watsuji, Western ethics (and concepts of self) that separate self from other, mind from body leads to "the standpoint of the isolated subjectivity, which abstracts from the practical connections between person and person, [and is then] forcibly applied to the questions of ethics."[41] To view ethics from such a standpoint is to not recognize that lived experience teaches us that the place of ethics is between people, as embodied subjects. And Watsuji goes even further, I believe, suggesting that cultivating a conception of human being as *ningen* is *inseparable* from living ethically with others.

Such a concept of self—one that includes all dimensions of human being-in-the-world—allows the ethical concepts of empathy and interconnectedness to resonate with a great deal more strength than merely a collection of individual isolated egos. On Watsuji's view, not only do we recognize that the other is *like* us, but due to the movement of negation in *ningen*, in the moment of emptiness, in nondualism, we in fact merge with the other—the self and other distinction empties out in betweenness; we are truly selfless and intimately connected with each other. Watsuji's efforts to redress the excessive emphasis on the importance of the individual in Western ethics can provide Western philosophy, with a framework for harnessing this powerful interconnectedness of all human beings.

Watsuji's view of human being as *ningen* is nondualistic then, in several respects. One such aspect is the nondualism of self and other; another is nondualism of bodymind. As Yuasa explains, in the Eastern way of thinking, examining the body is not an isolated area of philosophical investigation: "Inquiring what the body is, or what the relationship between the mind and body is, relates to the nature of being human."[42] By this he means that an investigation of the concept of body is at the same time an investigation of self, of being-in-the-world. How different this is from the disembodied, individuated, authentic Da-sein that we find in Heidegger's philosophy, and stronger still than what we saw even in Husserl. If we recall the earlier examples of the attraction between mother and baby, and the desire to be physically with one's friend or lover, not only the fact of, but also the *power* of this interconnectedness and interdependence is recognized. But it does not follow that we must or should give up all of the aspects of an individual, independent self. In chapters 4 and 5 I will return to this idea to see how this seeming tension can be addressed when we integrate feminist philosophies and Japanese philosophies.

While Watsuji's philosophy holds that as human beings we are *ningen* and thus ethical, this is still something that needs to be cultivated. In the next section we will look at Yuasa's theory of self-cultivation in relation to our being as *ningen*.

Yuasa's Theory of the Body

In the preface to *The Body: Towards an Eastern Mind-Body Theory* Yuasa points out that different questions concerning the body-mind relationship are given priority in the Eastern and Western traditions. In the East, he says, priority is given to the questions "'How does the relationship between the mind and the body *come to be* (through cultivation)?' or 'What does it *become*?'"[43] Typically in the West, however, the question is "'What *is* the relationship between the mind-body?"[44] For Yuasa, this indicates that the primary concern in the East is one of lived understanding of the mind-body relationship prior to a theoretical understanding. He contrasts this with the approach in Western philosophy which puts priority on abstract, theoretical understanding. In Yuasa's philosophy the phrase of the medieval Zen master Eisai, "the oneness of body-mind" (*shinjin ichinyo* 身心一如) best expresses the nonduality of bodymind in Japanese philosophy. In Japanese thought, even though nonduality is a capacity we all have, after all, as we have seen it is a inherent part of being human as *ningen*, it is still something we need to cultivate. Cultivation "embraces a characteristic that is a method of developing and enhancing a potential capacity with which everyone is generally endowed."[45] Self-cultivation, on Yuasa's view, be it Daoist practice, traditional Chinese medicine, martial arts, the art of the sword, yoga or poetry, involves cultivation of *ki* energy and leads to wisdom that is neither lodged in a purely intellectual faculty, i.e., it is not propositional, nor in purely physical dispositions nor in any straightforward combination of the two.

Ki is the vital force that pervades all life. As Shigenori Nagatomo explains in the introduction to *The Body, Self-Cultivation, and Ki-Energy*, *ki* has a broad scope and "can include, for example, a climatic condition, an arising social condition, a psychological and pathological condition. It also extends to cover a power expressed in fine arts, martial arts, and literature."[46] According to Yuasa, *ki* energy has "a *psychophysical* character that cannot be properly accommodated within the dualistic paradigm of thinking."[47] Rather, cultivation of *ki* subverts the Western distinction between body and mind. *Ki* is not something that is experienced *only* intellectually—in fact, the point is that in order to truly understand *ki* and be able to harness this vital force, one must realize that "it is not arrived at merely through intellectual abstraction, but is derived also from the observation of empirical phenomena detectable both experientially and experimentally in and around the human body."[48] It is something that is within our own embodied selves and also extends beyond our bodies even as it remains a part of them. It is an all-encompassing notion; it permeates our entire way of being-in-the-world and is at odds with the view of body as mere matter and as isolated from other bodies. Yuasa puts it this way: "The scientific study of *ki* . . . suggests through its biological and physical energy measurement of the living human body that there latently exists an invisible exchange of life between the living human body and the environment, that is, between a human being and the world, which transcends the surface relation established through consciousness and sensory perception."[49] It follows that this exchange of life also occurs between human bodies as well. *Ki* might well be the active aspect of Watsuji's self-active body.[50]

For Watsuji and Yuasa, through cultivation the human being comes to attain knowledge that is integrated in the bodymind—body and mind come to know together, as an integrated whole. We see, then, how such ethics could never be based *purely* on rationality. Yuasa devotes a chapter of *The Body: Toward an Eastern Mind-Body Theory* to the question "What is cultivation?" The Japanese term for cultivation, *shugyō* (修行), is also the term for Buddhist practice and focuses, as we will see in examples below, on training the mind through the body with the ultimate goal being the attainment of their oneness, for when we attain oneness of bodymind it is also the same moment of dissolution of the other dualities and we become selfless, open and ethical. Referring to Watsuji's *The Practical Philosophy of Early Buddhism* (*Genshi bukkyō no jissentetsugaku, Zenshū*, vol. 5), Yuasa tells us that in fact, Watsuji maintained that Buddhism taught that the only true cognition is that which comes through practice. As Yuasa explains,

> when one cognizes the mode of the Being of beings in the state of non-ego, one will be able to know the configuration and the meaning of the real. This cognition—that is, the 'observation of *dharmas* in no-ego'—unfolds only through 'practice to reach the state of no-ego.' Consequently, there is no separation here between cognition and practice. 'Herein we find a cognition that does not distinguish the theoretical from the practical, that is, a cognition of actuality itself. It is this which characterizes philosophical cognition in Buddhism.'[51]

We can read body in Buddhism as just as much of an epistemological site as the mind—in fact, true knowledge is their integration in bodymind—where there is no difference made between theoretical and practical cognition. What Yuasa means regarding cognition or theory not being separate from practice is that the knowledge gained through self-cultivation is not simply propositional knowledge—the knowledge usually associated with theory. Rather this kind of cognition is a mastery integrated in the bodymind through cultivation and practice as well as theoretical knowledge at the same time—it is lived and hence embodied knowledge. Mastery or true knowledge, or pure experience of something, means "becoming a thing and exhausting it" and this is accomplished when "the mind becomes completely one with the body as thing."[52] Yet we should not understand this "thing" as being a static object. Rather what Yuasa attempts to describe here is the integration of bodymind. Yuasa explains Nishida Kitaro's idea of becoming a thing as follows:

> through practice, the mind extinguishes the self-consciousness as a subject op-posing the body and its objectivity; the mind becomes completely one with the body as thing. At this point, the body loses its objectivity as a thing and, as it were, is made subjective. This way of being a subject is not the self-consciousness grounded in the *basho* vis-à-vis being, but is the self qua *basho* in the *basho* vis-à-vis nothing, that is, 'the self without being a self.'[53]

Once more we notice the movement of negation present in Watsuji's *ningen* in this description of bodymind knowledge. This is a very different starting point than what took root in much of the Western tradition. There, as Grosz points out, "[i]t could be argued that philosophy as we know it has established itself as a form of knowing, a form of rationality, only through the disavowal of the body, specifically the male body, and the correspond-ing elevation of mind as a disembodied term."[54] On these terms, knowledge was equated with coming to know which propositional claims were true and which were false. From the perspective of Watsuji, Yuasa, and feminist phi-losophers such as Elizabeth Grosz, such philosophy can only offer a limited and partial account of knowledge.

Looking closely at how the person is conceptualized in Zen Buddhism, however, echoes of which we see in Watsuji's account of *ningen*, can show us a more complete account of knowledge, inclusive of the body. In Zen Buddhism, the person is seen as a psychophysical unity; it is a nondualistic notion of person, which allows for Hakuin's statement that "this very body is the Buddha." In Zen, *satori* or enlightenment, the pinnacle of knowledge, is not possible through the intellect alone; rather *zazen*, seated meditation, is necessary—the oneness of bodymind must be cultivated. As Yuasa explains, theoretical understanding of the notion of unity is not enough. The body must live it as well: "The ordinary understanding is that cultivation is practical training aimed at the development and enhancement of one's spirit or personality. . . . Eastern thought traditionally tends to emphasize the inseparability of mind and body. Therefore, personal cultivation in the East takes on the meaning of a practical project aiming at the enhancement of the personality and the training of the spirit by means of the body."[55] Here in fact, the body, in the process of self-cultivation, is used to enhance the knowledge gained through the intellect to come to a fuller understanding whereby the knowledge can be embodied and lived.

This nondualistic knowledge that integrates the theoretical and practical is known as the "right mind" or "one-mind-ness" and one way this is cultivated in the Zen tradition is through meditation, which is largely a *bodily* activity. This right mind, or "one-mind," it is important to note, cannot in any way be equated with the mind in Descartes' mind-body dualism—it is not an entity or a substance, but a way of being: "the one-mind is an integration of, and a comprehensive whole of, both the unconscious and the body. When this integration is achieved through the process of self-cultivation, the three terms, 'one-mind,' 'the unconscious,' and 'the body' are interchangeable."[56] Theoretical or conceptual understanding is not enough—the body must learn as well. As Yuasa explains, this is done through cultivation. While in our everyday life the mind may dominate the body, in meditation, the ultimate goal of which, as put by Zen master Dōgen, is "body-mind molting and falling off,"[57] at first the body dominates the mind. Yuasa explains:

> meditative thinking first puts the body prior to the mind by letting the former comply with a set form. By setting up such an artificial situation, one realizes that the everyday understanding of the self is inauthentic. We are led to experience that the body, as the determination of the human subject, is an object that does not originally belong to the sovereignty of rational consciousness.[58]

Here in what Yuasa describes, we see how meditation integrates the body and the mind and arrives at the realization that we are in fact, bodymind. For Dōgen, once we become fully integrated, then we can move beyond even this. Again we see here a connection with the emptiness inherent in *ningen*. In fact, Watsuji explains this in quite extreme terms in *Ethics* in his discussion of Buddhism and the molting and falling off of bodymind. Here he is explaining how even human bodies are not ultimately, isolated from one another. He notes: "When they break through this bodily meditation, their body becomes entirely emptied. That is to say, the subjective body terminates in absolute emptiness, when its individuality is carried to the extreme."[59] It is in emptiness, we recall, that we find the between, infused with *ki* energy, which is the place where our bodies connect with one another. The recognition that fully experiencing the between, the *ki*, involves *all* aspects of our human embodied being-in-the-world and paves the way for a deeper interconnection and knowledge not only of ourselves, but also for a deeper interconnection with and knowledge of other human beings, and the world itself.

As a result, the body is an inseparable aspect of ethical being-in-the-world. Yuasa discusses the link inherent in Asian thought between ethical living and meditative practice. Referring to Watsuji's book on early Buddhism, Yuasa notes that "[w]hat is most necessary for humanity is not theoretical speculation, but, rather, the practice that eliminates delusions from one's own soul and detaches one from egoism."[60] The practice he refers to here is cultivation of bodymind.

As Yuasa explains in his discussion of Nishida's philosophy, detachment from egoism, emptying one's self, results in a "greatly expanded personality" that is emptied of all ego-concerns and reveals immediate knowledge and truth.[61] In his discussion of Dōgen, Yuasa emphasizes that the "fundamental attitude in cultivating the Way of the Buddhas is to reverse the ordinary thinking that places the mind (spirit) above the body. This emphasis on the body captures the meaning of cultivation for Dōgen as well as for Buddhism in general."[62] Such a placing of the body as a central part of enlightenment and ethics requires a complete reconfiguring of ethics as traditionally conceived of in the West.

Yuasa suggests that in fact, the mind-body dualism prevalent in Western philosophy can actually have dangerous consequences. For him the preoccupation with and reification of science and technology in the West are evidence of the emphasis put on knowledge gained solely through the mind that lacks the bodily or practical dimension. On his analysis, science and technology have become *the* sole modes of modern knowledge, and his work argues for a re-orientation of our conceptual grid and ways of knowing—for the current ("Western") grid covers over the body.[63] As he explains, "modern science has studied the living organism, including the human being, as an object of its research and attempted to manipulate it."[64] Modern science has taken mind-body dualism to an extreme here. Again, taking as central the ideas of bodymind oneness and Dōgen's "the molting of body-mind," Yuasa maintains that "when the dualistic and ambiguous tension in the relationship between the mind and body is dissolved, and the ambiguity overcome, a new perspective—what may be called the disclosed horizon (*Offenheit*)—will come into view."[65] This is a horizon out of which ethical being-in-the-world will naturally spring. However, this horizon can only come into view through cultivation, which aims at this new perspective, and is the method that "awakens and develops the psychophysiological potential that every human being possesses."[66]

This kind of horizon, the knowledge that this perspective brings to light makes the theoretical or conceptual inseparable from the practical. As Yuasa puts it: "In traditional Eastern metaphysics, there is, then, no sharp demarcation between the metaphysical and the physical dimensions. They are two mutually permeating regions in a continuum; cultivation is a process in which one's soul progresses gradually from the physical to the metaphysical dimension."[67] Such a process is intimately linked with a movement to the ethical, such that it becomes a way of being-in-the-world; ethical living becomes the nature of the reality of being human.

The examples Yuasa points to in his discussion of the role of body in both Watsuji and Nishida, indicate that discussion of the body—or bodymind—is always about ethics, or that ethics is always in the background of such a discussion:

> Masculinity and femininity designate psychological personality traits when seen from the ethical standpoint, i.e., various virtues. . . . It is the ideal to *embody* these virtues regardless of whether one is a male or female. However, these virtues have their foundations not in the self-centered ego standpoint, but in the standpoint of the nothingness of ego-consciousness, and consequently, in the other-centered standpoint in which the self sacrifices itself in the interpersonal relationship.[68]

This is, I maintain, in harmony with Watsuji's ethics of betweenness, echoes the dynamic nature of *ningen* and illustrates the embodiment of whole personhood—not making "male" or "female" distinctions, an idea to which we will return in chapter 5. As we saw in the earlier discussion of *ningen* one's self is momentarily lost, sacrificed in the between in order to reemerge as individual once more.

We can begin to imagine how much our view of the world might change if we take Yuasa's vision of human being-in-the-world seriously, and begin to cultivate it ourselves. He explains,

> we can discover a path that moves from psychology to ethics. In short, the ultimate goal of meditation is to cast off a state where instincts issue forth with ego-consciousness as their center, and where there lies the continuous deconstructing and reconstructing of the psychological structure of personality.[69]

Such a dynamic notion of self and body (reminiscent of Watsuji's theory of human being as *ningen*), one that connects us to all other beings gives us an ethical orientation for being-in-the-world. Taking Yuasa's philosophy further, body can become the place for ethics—dynamic, shifting, involving constant reflection and action—a site for moral praxis.

Bodymind, betweenness, *ningen*, and even the very idea of a "knowing body" all challenge our dualistic ways of thinking. Such experiences are nondual, and thanks to our Cartesian heritage, we tend, I think, to try to make sense of non-dual experience by thinking of it as an experience of "body + mind," of body as a manifestation of an inner mind or as guided by it. Even when the mind is conceived of as lodged in the brain it is still thought of as a capacity apart from the body. This does not, however fully capture the concept of the bodymind as epistemological site. One explanation for this difficulty that has been suggested is that we lack vocabulary for such a notion because we have no framework for making sense of this Asian concept. As David Loy explains: "the claim of sub-ject-object nonduality has been a seed which, however often sown, has never found fertile soil, because it has been too antithetical to those other vigorous sprouts that have grown into modern science and technology."[70] Indeed,

> Because nonduality is so incompatible with our usual experience—or, as the nondualist usually prefers, with our usual way of understanding experience—it is very difficult to grasp what exactly is meant when it is claimed that, for example, perception is or can be nondual. . . . But that nonduality is difficult to understand is necessarily true, according to the various systems which assert it. If we did understand it fully we would be enlightened, which is not understanding in the usual sense: it is the experience of non-duality which philosophizing obstructs. From such a perspective, the problem with philosophy is that its attempt to grasp nonduality conceptually is inherently dualistic and thus self-defeating.[71]

As long as we continue to seek *conceptual* understanding of bodymind, we will not be able to make sense of it. This does not mean, however, that we should give up. As Thomas Kasulis suggests, in order to understand nondualism, "we have to reorient the grids by which we have traditionally understood the world."[72] In the next two chapters, we will see how feminist philosophy has contributed to such reorientation.

Notes

1. Watsuji, *Ethics*, 68.
2. Husserl, *Cartesian*, 121.

3. Edmund Husserl, *Ideas Pertaining to a Pure Phenomenology and to a Phenomeno-logical Philosophy: Second Book: Studies in the Phenomenology of Constitution.* Trans. R. Rojcewicz and A. Schuwer. Dordrecht: Kluwer, 1989. Trans. of *Ideen zu einer Reinen Phänomenologie und Phänomenologischen Philosophie: Zweites Buch: Phänomenologische Untersuchungen zur Konstitution. Husserliana,* vol. IV. Ed. Marly Biemel. The Hague: Martinus Nijhoff, 1952, 35. "Bodies" is the translation of *Leib* (see translator's intro-duction to *Ideas II*). The translation suggested by Dorion Cairns however, in *Guide for Translating Husserl,* is "animate organism." However, another accepted transla-tion is "lived body;" see Elizabeth Behnke, "Edmund Husserl's Contribution to the Phenomenology of the Body in *Ideas II,*" in *Issues in Husserl's Ideas II* (Dordrecht: Kluwer, 1996), 138–139.

4. Richard Zaner, *The Problem of Embodiment: Some Contributions to the Phenom-enology of the Body* (The Hague: Martinus Nijhoff, 1964), vii.

5. David Loy, *Nonduality: A Study in Comparative Philosophy* (New Haven: Yale U.P., 1988), 21.

6. Husserl, *Ideas II,* 36.

7. Husserl, *Ideas II,* 172.

8. Husserl, *Ideas II,* 176.

9. Husserl, *Ideas II,* 174.

10. Elizabeth Spelman, "Woman as Body: Ancient and Contemporary Views," *Feminist Studies* 8.1 (Spring 1982): 111.

11. Drew Leder, "A Tale of Two Bodies: The Cartesian Corpse and the Lived Body," in *Body and Flesh: A Philosophical Reader,* ed. Donn Welton (Oxford: Black-well, 1998), 117.

12. Leder, "A Tale," 119.

13. Watsuji, *Ethics,* 65.

14. David Edward Shaner, *The Bodymind Experience in Japanese Buddhism: A Phe-nomenological Study of Kūkai and Dōgen* (Albany: SUNY Press, 1985), 99.

15. See Shaner, *The Bodymind,* particularly chapter 2 for an in-depth discussion of this concept.

16. Elizabeth Grosz, *Volatile Bodies: Toward a Corporeal Feminism* (Bloomington and Indianapolis: Indiana University Press, 1994), 4.

17. Grosz, *Volatile,* 5.

18. See Iris Marion Young, *On Female Body Experience: "Throwing like a Girl" and Other Essays* (Oxford: Oxford University Press, 2005), 5.

19. Shaner, *Bodymind,* 121; citation from Yoshito Hakeda, *Kūkai: Major Works* (New York: Columbia University Press, 1972), 89.

20. Yuasa Yasuo, "Cultivation of the Body in Japanese Religions," trans. Shigenori Nagatomo (unpublished essay given to the author by Yuasa), 17–18. The key ele-ment to note here is the resonance of Yuasa's analysis of the lack of the feminine voice in Western philosophy—this is not to say that there are not problems with depth psychology from a feminist perspective, but the key here is Yuasa's critique

of the Western philosophical tradition's emphasis on rationality and the resulting dichotomies that get put into place as given.

21. Grosz, *Volatile*, 5.

22. Shaner, *Bodymind*, 148.

23. Yuasa, "Cultivation," 13.

24. Parts of this section of the chapter are based on Erin McCarthy, "Towards Peaceful Bodies," in *Philosophieren über den Krieg: War in Eastern and Western Philosophies* (Berlin: Parerga, 2008), 147–164.

25. Watsuji, *Climate*, 11.

26. Watsuji, *Climate*, 11.

27. Yuasa Yasuo *The Body: Toward an Eastern Mind-Body Theory*, trans. Nagatamo Shigenori and T. P. Kasulis (Albany: SUNY, 1987), 47.

28. Watsuji, *Ethics*, 62.

29. Watsuji, *Ethics*, 62.

30. Watsuji, *Ethics*, 238.

31. Watsuji, *Ethics*, 10.

32. Yuasa, *The Body: Toward an Eastern*, 39. *Basho*, for Yuasa's purposes here, simply means a physical place. However, it is also a technical term in modern Japanese philosophy, particularly in the work of Nishida Kitaro. See the editor's note on p. 38 of *The Body*.

33. Watsuji, *Ethics*, 65.

34. Watsuji, *Ethics*, 60.

35. Watsuji, *Ethics*, 12. See also my "Ethics in the Between," *Philosophy, Culture and Traditions* 2 (2003): 63–78, upon which parts of this chapter are based.

36. Watsuji, *Ethics*, 66.

37. Watsuji, *Ethics*, 66.

38. Watsuji, *Ethics*, 66.

39. Behnke, "Edmund Husserl's Contribution," 156.

40. Watsuji, *Ethics*, 64.

41. Watsuji, *Ethics*, 9.

42. Yuasa, *The Body: Toward an Eastern*, 24.

43. Yuasa, *The Body: Toward an Eastern*, 18.

44. Yuasa, *The Body: Toward an Eastern*, 18.

45. Yuasa, "Cultivation," 14.

46. Shigenori Nagatomo, "Translators Introduction," in Yuasa Yasuo, *The Body, Self Cultivation and Ki-Energy*, trans. Shigenori Nagatomo and Monte S. Hull (Albany: SUNY Press, 1993), xi.

47. Nagatomo, "Translator's Introduction," xii.

48. Nagatomo, "Translator's Introduction," xii.

49. Yuasa Yasuo, *The Body, Self Cultivation and Ki-Energy*, trans. Shigenori Nagatomo and Monte S. Hull (Albany: SUNY Press, 1993), 1.

50. See Erin McCarthy, "The Knowing Body," in *Sagesse du corps*, ed. Gabor Cspregi (Aylmer: Éditions du Scribe, 2001) for more on *ki*.

51. Yuasa, *The Body: Toward an Eastern*, 86–87.

52. Yuasa, *The Body: Toward an Eastern*, 70.

53. Yuasa, *The Body Toward an Eastern*, 70.

54. Grosz, *Volatile*, 4.

55. Yuasa, *The Body: Toward an Eastern*, 85.

56. Shigenori Nagatomo and Gerald Leisman, "An East Asian Perspective of Mind-Body," *The Journal of Medicine and Philosophy*, 21 (1996): 445.

57. Yuasa, *The Body: Toward an Eastern*, 118.

58. Yuasa, *The Body: Toward an Eastern*, 122.

59. Watsuji, *Ethics*, 67–68.

60. Yuasa, *The Body: Toward an Eastern*, 86.

61. Yuasa, *The Body: Toward an Eastern*, 65.

62. Yuasa, *The Body: Toward an Eastern*, 119.

63. Kasulis, "Editor's Introduction" to *The Body*, Yuasa Yasuo (Albany: SUNY, 1987), 1.

64. Yuasa, "A Contemporary Scientific Paradigm and the Discovery of the Inner Cosmos," *Self as Body in Asian Theory and Practice*, eds. T. P. Kasulis, R. Ames and W. Dissanayake, (Albany: SUNY Press, 1993), 348.

65. Yuasa, *The Body: Toward an Eastern*, 28.

66. Yuasa "Cultivation," 2.

67. Yuasa *The Body: Toward an Eastern*, 217.

68. Yuasa "Sexuality and Meditation," unpublished paper given to the author by Yuasa, 16.

69. Yuasa, "Sexuality," 16.

70. Loy, *Nonduality*, 3.

71. Loy, *Nonduality*, 5. Loy points out one of the central problems in attempting to discuss the idea of nondualism. Nondualism as used here refers generally to the Buddhist sense of *sunyata* or "nothingness" which overcomes "Cartesian" dualism while yet maintaining distinctions. ("Dualism" is used to express the Cartesian notion as it has permeated Western philosophy.)

72. Kasulis, introduction to *The Body*, 3.

CHAPTER FOUR

~

Toward an Embodied Ethics of Care

In both Japanese and feminist philosophies we find concepts of self that provide alternatives to the concept of self as the autonomous, isolated individual, and the ethics that results from such a conception of self. When the relational aspect of selfhood is foregrounded, when being in relation is recognized as an integral part of what it is to be a human being-in-the-world, then, as we will see, we are moving toward an ethics of care—an intimacy-oriented ethics, as Kasulis might put it—one that, as we will see, has relationality at its core. Robert Carter suggests that this view of self and the views of ethics associated with it characterize much of Asian philosophy—that "Taoism, and Zen Buddhism, and Buddhism teach us that we are intrinsically interrelated, and the ground of ethics and the foundation of ethical sentiment is the selfless recognition that we are each other's hopes and aspirations, sufferings and disappointments."[1] We will see that the feminist ethics of care shares key elements with this focus on relationality and interdependence that we find in Asian philosophy generally and in Watsuji's philosophy specifically.

Care Ethics: East and West

As we saw in chapter 1, in *Intimacy or Integrity: Philosophy and Cultural Difference*, Kasulis proposes a very useful way of thinking about different ways of relating, knowing and being-in-the-world, suggesting that there are two orientations of being-in-the-world—intimacy oriented and integrity oriented. He also notes that no one culture is ever a perfect example of only one orientation—both can be found in most cultures, although with varying degrees of emphasis. A feminist ethics of care lends itself more to the intimacy model, but also contains aspects of the integrity orientation, as one of the key concerns for feminist philosophy is to be sure to maintain women's autonomy.

Let us move to our specific examples of what we might call more intimacy-oriented ethics. We know that Watsuji's definition of human being as *ningen* includes self as both individual and relational, as well as embodied. And we recall that for Watsuji, one cannot be fully human, nor ethical (for if one is a human being in one's fullest potential, one is also ethical), unless one is, as well as being an individual, also in relation with other human beings. An ethics of care describes the self in a way strikingly similar to Watsuji's description. And while care ethics has changed significantly in the last thirty years, the concept of self that it seeks to foster and sees as central to its ideals has remained constant. Two of the earliest and most significant contributors to care ethics are Carol Gilligan and Nel Noddings. Gilligan's *In a Different Voice: Psychological Theory and Women's Development* famously suggested that girls approached moral problems from a different perspective than that of boys. Critical of Lawrence Kohlberg's theory of moral development for being based only on a study of boys and Kohlberg's conclusion that girls' moral development lags behind that of boys, Gilligan studied girls' and women's moral development. Her conclusions suggested that women and girls placed more importance on relationships and context than boys, who, according to Kohlberg's theory, ended up more frequently at what he alleges is the highest level of moral reasoning—the level that appeals to abstract principles and rules. While Gilligan's work has proven to be quite problematic in some ways for some feminists, there is widespread agreement that her work did serve to identify basic notions in the ethics of care which had previously been overlooked in the discourse of morality and viewed as philosophically insignificant. Until Gilligan's book, the kind of moral reasoning that was used by women—over half the population—had been left entirely out of the picture.

In her introduction to *Caring: A Feminine Approach to Ethics and Moral Education*, Noddings pursues the direction Gilligan opened up. There she argues that "[e]thics has been discussed largely in the language of the father: in principles and propositions, in terms such as justification, fairness, justice. The mother's voice has been silent."[2] By the mother's voice, she means, as we will see, the voice of receptivity, relatedness and responsiveness. If we make space for this voice, we find an alternative to the rational autonomous being of liberal individualism typical of an ethics rooted in an integrity orientation. This does not mean, however, that reason and autonomy are thrown out altogether. Rather, Watsuji's and Noddings's philosophies, and the philosophy of care ethics in general propose a *different* way of conceptualizing autonomy and independence, and also suggest that there may be a different kind of logic at work in moral decision making viewed from the care perspective. Her view is founded on her concept of a relational being and is one that acknowledges the necessity of interdependence for human survival and flourishing. This interdependence involves seeing oneself not as primarily separate from others, rather, as belonging in a network of relationships that support one's autonomy. In the same introduction, she adds that "[h]uman caring and the memory of caring and being cared for which I shall argue form the foundation of ethical response, have not received attention."[3] She further argues that while an ethics of care is a fundamentally feminine view, it is not limited to women. Here her view parts company with what Gilligan's research has been interpreted to imply. For Gilligan too, did not believe that caring only belonged to women. Most of us, after all, can recall being cared for, and those who were not cared for are deeply affected by its absence. "It is feminine," she says, "in the deeply classical sense—rooted in receptivity, relatedness and responsiveness."[4]

Writing over twenty years after Noddings, Virginia Held, in her 2006 book *The Ethics of Care: Personal, Political, and Global*, says that while maintaining "that the ethics of care has moved far beyond" its original foundations, its ". . . central focus . . . is [still] on the compelling moral salience of attending to and meeting the needs of the particular others for whom we take responsibility."[5] The concept of person that provides the starting point for her ethics of care is understood "as relational, rather than as the self-sufficient independent individuals of the dominant moral theories."[6] According to Held, an ethics of care "sees persons as interdependent, morally and epistemologically. Every person starts out as a child dependent on those providing us care, and we remain interdependent with others in thoroughly fundamental ways throughout our life. That we can think and act as if we were independent depends on a network of relations making it possible for us to do so. And our relations are part of what constitute our identity."[7] It is here where we begin to see the similarities with Watsuji's concept of *ningen*, and furthermore how this goes beyond the notions of intersubjectivity and interdependence that we found in Heidegger and Husserl.

There are differences with Watsuji's view, to be sure, and it is quite certain that Watsuji had no notion of feminist philosophy, but nonetheless, there are resonances with an ethics of care. For Watsuji, Noddings and Held, we are always already in relation. Both the self as Watsuji's *ningen* and the self of an ethics of care evoke the concept of interrelation, which is at the core of human being-in-the-world. As Watsuji's notion of *ningen* takes relation as fundamental to the self, so does an ethics of care. As Noddings puts it, "[t]aking relation as ontologically basic simply means that we recognize human encounter and affective response as a basic fact of human existence."[8] For an ethics of care and Watsuji's philosophy, it is this relation, this basic fact of human being-in-the-world that obliges us to care for the other. Due to the interdependent nature of being human where the other is a part of the self, self-care becomes other care and other care becomes self-care. We can no longer look at the other as something entirely isolated from ourselves and thus, realizing our deep interconnectedness, we cannot ignore the other's pain or suffering as it is also our own. Contrasting this to the ethics that arises out of an integrity orientation, that in some sense sees relatedness as not essential or constitutive of the self, Held states: "The ethics of care is, instead, hospitable to the relatedness of persons. It sees many of our responsibilities as not freely entered into but presented to us by the accidents of our embeddedness in familial and social and historical contexts. It often calls on us to take responsibility, while liberal individualist morality focuses on how we should leave each other alone."[9] Like Watsuji, Noddings and Held both use the mother-child and family relationships as, in their best instances, exemplary of the foundations of caring and relatedness, placing importance on this embeddedness in their discussions of basic ethical principles. As we saw in chapter 2, Watsuji uses the example of the mother and child in *Ethics* as a key example for demonstrating how such relationships and embeddedness, define us and determine our responsibilities. Here we also see a somewhat Confucian echo in Watsuji's philosophy.[10] While we will not go into detail here, in Confucian philosophy, relationality is also foundational for ethics and it too resonates with care ethics.[11] In Watsuji's work, as well as seeing this influence in the concept of *ningen*, we can also see it particularly expressed in his discussion of the family. As Graham Mayeda points out, "the family is a prescriptive ethical ideal in Confucian thought."[12] As mother or father, for example, one must obey certain rules and adhere to certain behaviors—those appropriate to the role one has in the family. Whether or not one has chosen such a role, as a parent, or spouse, or sibling, one takes on a certain responsibility to others in the family due to this "accident of embeddedness."[13] As soon as the family comes into being then, one is in this betweenness—implicated in a network of ethical relationships and its attendant moral obligations and entitlements. Watsuji, as we saw in chapter 1, extends these ideas to social relationships generally. As human beings, he explains, "we cannot first presuppose individuals, and then explain the establishment of social relationships among them. Nor can we presuppose society and from there explain the occurrence of individuals. Neither the one nor the other has 'precedence.'"[14] For him, the ethical structure of being human in society reflects the fundamental interdependence that care ethics also stresses.

Care Ethics and the Body

In his discussions of the examples of friendship and the mother-child relationship, Watsuji underlines both the interdependence and the caring that we find in an ethics of care and introduces something that I believe has not been introduced fully enough into the discussion of an ethics of care—that this interdependence cannot be understood as disembodied. Recall the citation from chapter 3 about a mother and her baby:

> A mother and her baby can never be conceived of as merely two independent individuals. . . . As is evident, a mother's body and her baby's are somehow connected as though one. . . . This power of attraction, even though not physical attraction alone, is yet a real attraction connecting the two as though one.[15]

Mother and child know one another bodily, not just physically (through mere recognition or as a source of nutrition and sustenance) and not psychologically (as a source of emotional support). They are not merely interdependent but bodily connected through caring or connected through bodily care—the point here being that the bodily word "connection" and the psychological word "care" are inseparable—the bodily connection is intrinsic to the caring relationship and not merely the means or manifestation of it. In the case of infancy described by Watsuji, of course, the active aspect of caring goes only one way. However, in this relationship there is the potential for reciprocity, which, as we will see shortly, is another key element of an ethics of care—it is reciprocal.

Watsuji's second example, we recall from chapter 3 is that of friendship: "That one wishes to visit a friend implies that she intends to draw near to the friend's body. If she does go to visit a friend who is at some distance by streetcar, then her body moves in the friend's direction, attracted by the power that draws them together."[16] Here we see the concept of interdependency of both bodies and minds—something that I think care ethics can benefit from integrating.[17] As Watsuji sees it, a relationship between two friends is not merely psychological. He maintains that the "mental" or "emotional" relation between two people cannot be understood apart from the "body" relation. We recall that Kasulis's list of aspects of the intimacy-oriented cultures, includes the somatic as well as the psychological. "Even when intimacy is not carnal (and usually it is not)," Kasulis stresses, "it is still incarnate. That is: human intimacy is embodied."[18] Watsuji's friendship example points out that when we are friends with someone we want to be near them, we want to be in their physical presence. There is something significant about being in the embodied presence of those with whom we are intimate. Even in the age of webcams and video conferencing, those encounters, even with our loved ones, still lack the intimacy of actually being with those we are close to. Intimacy-oriented ways of being-in-the-world, then, also recognize the importance of embodiment to human relationships of all kinds. As Kasulis explains, "intimacy is an incorporating [from the Latin, *incorporat*, embodied]: a drawing into the body. . . . We enter into intimate relations by opening ourselves to let the other inside, by putting ourselves into internal relations with others or recognizing internal relations that already exist."[19] Intimacy, he says, involves an incorporating of the other, drawing the other into the body. And this happens even in relations we might not usually consider intimate. Take the example of a sports team. Kasulis uses the example of a sportswriter writing about a "gloom-filled locker room" following a defeat, reminding us that in order to understand the atmosphere in the locker room, one must be an insider, a part of the team: "If one is restricted to the detached observer's standpoint, one cannot know this significance of the room as the team directly experiences its internal relation to it."[20] This example expresses the affective aspect of the intimacy orientation. It is easy now to also see how the members of the team are interdependent, how their identity as members of the team includes the belonging-with we discussed in chapter 2. In addition, even in the "gloom-filled locker room" there is an embodied aspect—this goes beyond the physical activity the teammates share—rather, as Kasulis puts it: "the experience of the players' gloom-filled locker room is inseparable from both the sensory (sights, sounds, smells) and the visceral (the hollow feeling in the pit of the abdomen)."[21] For Watsuji, too, we experience this in our normal, everyday existence and this further links us to others. A human body, he explains "is not, of its own accord, something individually independent. To make it individually independent we must cut its connections with other human bodies and completely dissociate it from its attraction to others."[22] For Watsuji as we saw in chapter 3, the movement of the body in the carrying out of ethical acts, for example, involves the integrated bodymind. As betweenness-oriented beings, as *ningen*, then, human bodies are ethically interconnected because they are both physically and mentally interconnected and vice versa. This is the place of caring, the place of ethics.[23]

Watsuji's concept of *ningen* as relational is also a key aspect that we find in the concept of self in care ethics. As Watsuji notes the complexity of negotiating roles in the family, for example, so care ethics takes into account our embeddedness in particular contexts. Here, as we will see later in the chapter, care ethics can correct the patriarchal slant of Watsuji's notion of familial relationships. Explicit in Watsuji, but implicit in care ethics, is that this relational self is also embodied. Adding a corporeal dimension to the theory of care ethics can strengthen the notion of relatedness inherent in the interdependent concept of self it promotes. For both Watsuji and care ethics, once we acknowledge this interdependence, obligation is immediate when faced with one in need of care.

Reciprocity

What is necessary in care ethics is also, as mentioned briefly above, however, at least the potential for reciprocity. For Wastuji, as we have seen, reciprocity arises out of the structure of *ningen*. The reciprocity in care ethics, however, adds a dimension we do not find in Watsuji's ethics. Here is a place where care ethics can enlighten and extend Wastuji's philosophy. For care ethics, including the notion of reciprocity, arises out of the concern to address the exploitation of women. For if we have care without reciprocity, the dangers of exploitation loom large. Held points out that since "even the helpful emotions can often become misguided or worse—as when excessive empathy with others leads to a wrongful degree of self-denial [or co-dependence] or when benevolent concern crosses over into controlling domination—we need an ethics of care, not just care itself. The various aspects and expressions of care and caring relations need to be subjected to moral scrutiny and evaluated, not just observed and described."[24] What can appear to be care may prove on closer inspection not to involve care at all, and indeed to be the opposite—not a matter of caring for the other, but for meeting one's own needs or soothing one's own anxieties—something that is self-referential and even selfish.[25] Held's examples of excessive self-denial and control in the guise of the benevolent concern are in the end both self-referential in this way. The potentially exploitative, self-referential aspect of care finds a parallel in the Japanese concept of *amae*, first brought to the attention of the psychoanalytic community by Takeo Doi in *The Anatomy of Dependence*.[26] As defined by Doi *amae* is "the desire to be passively loved"[27] or "passive dependence, or passive love."[28] In Japan, *amae* is generally accepted as an important part of child development. Faith Bethelard and Elizabeth Young-Bruehl translate *amae* as "cherishment" and demonstrate how, for Doi, care and the need for care are fundamental to human being. As they put it, Doi "proposed that the infant begins in a condition of relatedness that is predominantly ego instinctual, not predominantly aggressive, or libidinal. The relation that Freud thought existed only between a mother and her male child is, in Doi's view, the norm."[29] Their suggestion here seems to be that the care instinct is primordial—that we come into the world fundamentally care oriented, reaching out to the other or, as Kasulis might say, intimacy oriented: "Infants want cherishing, and caretakers, if they are cherishers, read the infant's preverbal signals and cherish them. The infant stretches out to the caretakers, in order to receive; the caretakers receive, hold, literally and intrapsychically, the infant and her needs, in order to give. They are a circuitry, like the symbol of infinity. Cherishment is the elemental form of reciprocity."[30] We notice here that the characterization of this kind of care includes the body as a key element and that they challenge Doi's characterization of *amae* as passive. As Young-Bruehl explains in a later article, which focuses on the adult manifestation of *amae* in love relationships: "In the *amae* state we say: I wish that your only wishes were to sweetly, indulgently love me and to receive my sweet and indulgent love! Cherish me, and I will cherish you! In the *amae* state we desire relationship, reciprocity, interplay. . . . The little lover feels the caretaker's love as such, as cherishing, caretaking; solicits its continuance; and gives in turn what he or she has felt."[31] On this view, we see again that part of what it is to be human is to be interdependent and how this web of interdependence is in place from the very beginning. From this view of the self it follows, as Watsuji puts it, that "ethics is not a matter of individual consciousness alone."[32] To view the self as something isolated, purely autonomous and individual—the view upon which so much philosophy is predicated—is from this standpoint, almost absurd and false to the way we live and grow. Still, this is not to say the notion of *amae* is a panacea or entirely benign. As Kazuko Behrens explains, there is a potentially exploitative aspect of *amae* that echoes the potential for exploitation also inherent in the idea of care. As she observes, *amae* "represents a cluster of behaviors, an emotional or internal state, and a philosophical construct for Japanese people that can be viewed either positively or negatively . . . [but] always consists of some expectation or assumption on the part of the *amae* doer of being understood and accepted, whether it is for pure affection or instrumental needs, either within intimate or non-intimate relationships."[33] Behrens goes on to discuss the fact that while *amae* behaviors are for the most part desired by both giver and receiver, there are cases of "manipulative *amae*." For example, to illustrate the use of *amae* after childhood, Behrens cites a woman from Tokyo who says, "I'm over thirty now but still live with my parents. I keep telling myself that I should leave home and be independent, but I am doing *amae* because of the convenience of having 'home.'"[34] This use of the term clearly contradicts Young-Bruehl's interpretation above. Behrens also provides evidence of husbands using "manipulative *amae*" toward their wives. As she explains, some Japanese men expect "things will get done without their involvement and expect their wives to understand what they want and comply with even unstated requests at times."[35] Behrens gives further examples of abuses of *amae* directed at women working in the corporate world. The potential for abuse of these notions leads Held to stress that an ethics of care that evaluates, rather than just describes, is necessary. Care ethics uses the idea of caring to address injustice of many kinds and has the potential to expand the power of such an ethics to address global and political problems.

As we saw in the previous chapter, if we focus only on concepts and definitions we miss the point. The concepts mean nothing if they are not put into practice, if they are not embodied and lived in the world. The aim is not to find necessary and sufficient conditions for defining good and bad care or for applying the concept in judgment. The aim is to cultivate care in one's self and one's relationships, hence the importance of the element of reciprocity in the ethics of care. To take what we saw in chapter 3 and build on it here, making oneself caring is a matter of cultivating selflessness, whether that be through meditation or yoga, or working to understand self as fundamentally interconnected with all other human beings. To use Kasulis's theory, in "the intimacy orientation, ethics demands that I open myself to the other and accept the opening of the other to me."[36] And, as we saw in Watsuji's description of *ningen*, this is something that continually shifts and changes. It is not a matter of determining a universal principle that can then be applied forever to all situations. Rather, such an ethics is responsive as one enters into the other's situation.[37] While the practices of care are many, Held maintains that "all care involves attentiveness, sensitivity, and responding to needs."[38] Like Watsuji's ethics, care ethics is a practical ethics which, Held maintains, can enrich an ethics of justice (or integrity to use Kasulis's term) and give it more force. A theory of equality, for example, does not do much good if those people for whom it is to help do not actually have their needs met. Referring to human rights, Held writes:

> The motive for including economic and social rights among the human rights on the grounds of justice is that it would be unfair and a failure of equality, especially of rights to equal freedom, not to do so. When meeting needs is

motivated by care, on the other hand, the needs themselves are responded to and the persons themselves with these needs are cared for.[39]

Notice that neither Watsuji's nor care ethics asks us to give up the values of integrity—which, we recall, include the notion of the independent individual. Rather, they maintain that such an ethics *on its own* does not fully meet the needs of human beings—especially those whose rights have been marginalized, ignored or even denied.

Global Care Ethics

Held maintains that the ethics of care can specifically work toward extending caring to the global social and political realms, further illustrating how an ethics developing out of the kind of selfhood we see cultivated in Watsuji's philosophy and care ethics, while having strong roots in feminism and serving to address the needs of women, does not apply only to women. It is the relational orientation at the foundation of this concept of self that obligates us to behave ethically within the network of our personal and familial relationships but also on a broader scale. If we begin, following Watsuji and care ethics, to rethink the concept of person as relational, we see that "we cannot refuse obligation in human affairs by merely refusing to enter relation; we are, by virtue of our mutual humanity, already and perpetually in potential relation."[40] In moving care ethics to the global, Held puts the emphasis on moving from caring individuals to these caring relations. Furthermore, we know, from what we have seen in Watsuji's ethics, and our brief discussion of Buddhism, that, on these views, all human beings are fundamentally interconnected, which gives further force to Held's project. Held points out that

> small societies of family and friendship embedded in larger societies are formed by caring relations. More attenuated but still evident caring relations between more distanced people enable them to trust each other enough to form social organizations and political entities and to accept each other as fellow citizens of states. A globalization of caring relations would help enable people of different states and cultures to live in peace, to respect each other's rights, to care together for their environments, and to improve the lives of their children.[41]

And here, we see that Noddings's earlier critique of liberal individualism in light of the ethics of care seems to resonate with Watsuji's. As Held puts it: "Moralities built on the image of the independent, autonomous, rational individual largely overlook the reality of human dependence and the morality for which it calls."[42] The reality of human dependence without morality results, often, in exploitation. In a dependent and interdependent world, the assumption of independence often leads to neglect or dependence wrongly viewed as the result of autonomous choices (rarely the case in poverty, for example). Ethics that focus solely on independence fail to recognize our fundamental interdependence—and that can lead to the legitimation of exploitation of those who are dependent.

What is clear in both Watsuji and the ethics of care is that one's individuality can be preserved even though essentially influenced and informed by an other. Recall Held's observation that our thinking and acting as if we were independent blind us to the fact that the self relies on and develops within a network of relations—and hence involves interdependence whether we recognize it or not. Yet despite this we don't feel as if we've completely lost a sense of self. In other words, having a unique identity and being interdependent is not a contradiction in terms in our lived experience. Even for Watsuji—for whom the self dissolves into community—the self likewise reemerges as individual, only to resume the process once more. This cycle is not merely repetition or a process that yields the same results. For him, the idea of repetition serves only to reinforce the starting and ending points of the cycle and is contrary to the movement of *ningen*. On his view, the self is dynamic, open, receptive, adaptive, and capable of responding to the new situations or people, as appropriate. This characterization fits Noddings's definition of caring, and Held's characterization above of what all care has in common. And while the features of the self it stresses—caring, relationship, interdependence—are often identified with the feminine, in Watsuji's work they are identified simply as human. As we saw previously in chapter 2, human beings as *ningen* continually negotiate their nondualism, moving fluidly between the individual and relational aspects of self, for we all "possess this dynamic structure of reciprocal transformation."[43]

The structure of *ningen* recognizes the interdependence that is critical to human flourishing in the globalized world. Watsuji recognizes that we as human beings are both individuals and in relation. And, as cited above, an ethics of care acknowledges this as well. Neither philosophy necessarily, as we have seen, denies the importance of autonomy. Rather they suggest only that autonomy is not to be understood apart from human relationships, that it is not to be understood apart from the body, that it is not the defining characteristic of a person nor necessarily the primary concept on which to build a moral theory or understand ethical experience. As noted, Held, like Watsuji, believes that relations partly constitute our identity—even our identity as autonomous beings. She writes: "This [to say we are interdependent] is not to say that we cannot become autonomous; feminists have done much interesting work developing an alternative conception of autonomy in place of the liberal individualist one. Feminists have much experience rejecting or reconstituting relational ties that are oppressive."[44] This aspect of her theory is important to add to Watsuji's in this constructive comparative enterprise.

So far I have been drawing heavily on the work of Virginia Held, but it is important to note some possible differences between her view and my own project here. She is, I would argue, one of the most prominent philosophers of care ethics today. It is clear from what I have said here and discussed elsewhere,[45] that I share her belief in the power of care ethics in a global context. I think bringing Watsuji's and Held's care ethics together gives us a model of selfhood that can be extended to create a model for international and cross cultural relations. Despite my sympathy for Held's project, however, I have some concerns that remain. I agree with, for example, her claim that "[w]e can, for instance, develop caring relations for persons who are suffering deprivation in distant parts of the globe. Moral theories that assume only individuals pursuing their own interests within the constraints supplied by universal rules [which too often are anything but] are ill-suited to deal with the values of caring relations and of relational persons."[46] I also agree when she asserts above that globalizing caring relations can help us connect with and care for those who are in distant locations. What is not so clear is whether Held would agree with me that the very sort of constructive comparative philosophy that I am engaged in can further the goals of an ethics of care. In the very article just cited she writes:

> Although there are similarities between the ethics of care and communitarianism, and between the ethics of care and Confucianism and what are sometimes thought of as "Asian values," many now argue that any satisfactory ethics of care, or perhaps even any ethic that deserves the name "ethics of care," will be a feminist ethics that includes an insistence on the equality of women, not one accepting a traditional gender hierarchy.[47]

As I have stated, I acknowledge that an ethics of care is a feminist project and agree firmly that it must be a feminist ethics. However, I also believe that this obligates us to take very seriously the idea of interdependence upon which an ethics of care is founded, especially if we want this sort of ethics to be relevant globally and also to advance us beyond the sort of traditional understanding of care that, as critics have pointed out for the last twenty years, reinforces the idea that women's concerns are limited to Kinder, Küche and Kirche. Turning to philosophies from other cultures that provide alternatives to the liberal individualist view of self and ethics—where not just women but all human beings are viewed relationally—can help address this critique of an ethics of care by enriching the fundamental notions of "self," "dependence," "autonomy," and "care" on which it depends. It seems to me, in fact, a natural extension of Held's theory to suppose that the attention to interdependence that she is out to cultivate must include attention to the interdependence of cultural and philosophical traditions—be they Confucian or, as I have suggested here, Watsujian. As I see it, Watsuji's thought provides proponents of care ethics with rich ways of thinking about the self that are inherently nondualistic, that resist the mind/body split. At the same time, I insist this comparative approach to an ethics of care remains a feminist project. Comparing the ethics of care with Watsuji's philosophy, forces us to confront its arguably patriarchal slant and to reflect on how this persists despite the model of self and ethics he promotes. This comparison may also provide a way of conceptualizing a knowing body that includes more than so-called female knowledge and in so doing, help to address critiques of feminist ethics of care that argue that care ethics serves to reinforce stereotypical concepts of women as caring nurturers whose place is in the private, not public, or philosophical spheres. Held maintains that "[t]o be acceptable, it [the ethics of care] must be a feminist ethic, open to both women and men to adopt. But in being feminist, it is different from the ethics of its precursors."[48] Again, here I agree with her entirely. In suggesting that Watsuji can be used to enrich feminist ethics of care and feminist ethics of care can be used to enrich Watsuji, I am not merely trying to slip feminist ethics in the back door of comparative philosophy. I am saying the comparison is essential to building constructive relations among people of diverse traditions. Nor am I claiming that Watsuji is in the end a feminist and that Watsuji and Held have identical philosophies. To the contrary. The very fact that he has an ethics similar to an ethics of care but no feminist consciousness is a fact of great importance and interest—something to be pondered and confronted. The very point of comparative philosophy of this kind is to explore the similarities and differences in order to see what each has to learn from the other. Nor am I claiming that because we can find notions of self and ethics central to feminist ethics of care in Japanese philosophy but applied there to all human beings, that these views are not really feminist views after all. What I am saying is that Watsuji does not draw the implications for concerns of feminist philosophers and that it is here that a feminist ethics of care has much to teach him. In short, I see comparative feminist philosophy of the kind I have been pursuing as concerned with building relationships, fostering the sort of interdependence Held seeks and engaging in critical exchange between two philosophies in an effort to promote the ethics Held defends. The exchange of ideas is itself an ethical enterprise and if care ethics is right, then the development of ethical ideals is itself relational and comparative. If we are truly concerned with addressing problems of both women and men globally, are we not also obliged by interdependence to look for links, to negotiate points in common with cultures other than our own and to begin to dialogue across differences? Held states that the "ethics of care builds on experience that all persons share, though they have often been unaware of its embedded values and implications."[49] Again, I agree with her. I would only like to add that there are philosophies, such as Watsuji's, wherein these embedded values have at least been recognized, indeed for centuries and some of these further implications already thought through. And while Watsuji and others have yet to consider questions of gender and feminist concerns, there is nothing to suggest that such concerns cannot be incorporated into new theories that can come out of such views.

Held says "that to include nonfeminist versions of valuing caring among the moral approaches called the ethics of care is to unduly disregard the history of how this ethics has developed and come to be a candidate for serious consideration among contemporary moral theories. The history of the development of the contemporary ethics of care is the history of recent feminist progress."[50] What is not clear to me is whether she assumes that the bridge between cultures that will allow care ethics to spread globally and—as she states in the concluding sentence of her book, "help enable people of different states and cultures to live in peace, to respect each other's rights, to care together for their environments, and to improve the lives of their children"[51]—is already built, and that the ethics of care as she formulates it is that bridge. Or whether, instead, her work invites, and indeed requires, comparison with relevant nonfeminist versions of caring in order to enhance, enrich and strengthen our understanding of what form a feminist care ethics should take? As I see it, without the latter sort of project, her version risks excluding other philosophical and cultural values and perspectives. From my standpoint as a comparative feminist philosopher, I see no reason not to incorporate ideas inspired by or found in nonfeminist conceptions of care into a global feminist ethics of care. Indeed doing so is imperative to building understanding across diverse cultural and philosophical traditions. As I see it, we are not left with an either/or proposition when it comes to feminism and comparative philosophy. In fact, we can adapt, adopt, and learn from such non-Western, nonfeminist ideas and incorporate them into our notions of care, while maintaining a feminist approach and commitment to feminist ethics. To proceed in this way, as I see it, encourages the feminist progress that Held so astutely and powerfully outlines and contributes to in her book.

The very project of a feminist ethics of care, with its call for recognizing and valuing interdependence, I believe requires that we move beyond our own philosophical culture to engage others in constructive dialogue.

Notes

An earlier version of this chapter appears in *Frontiers of Japanese Philosophy II: Neglected Themes and Hidden Variations*, ed. Victor Hori and Melissa Curley (Nagoya: Nanzan Institute for Religion and Culture, 2008), 113–128.

1. Robert E. Carter, *Encounter with Enlightenment: A Study of Japanese Ethics* (Albany: SUNY Press, 2001), 32.
2. Noddings, *Caring: A Feminine Approach to Ethics and Moral Education* (Berkeley: University of California Press, 1984), 1.
3. Noddings, *Caring*, 1.
4. Noddings, *Caring*, 2.
5. Virginia Held, *The Ethics of Care: Personal, Political, and Global* (New York: Oxford University Press, 2006), 10.
6. Held, *Ethics of Care*, 13.
7. Held, *Ethics of Care*, 13–14.
8. Noddings, *Caring*, 4.
9. Held, *Ethics of Care*, 14–15.
10. For more on the Confucian influence in Watsuji's thought see Steve Odin, "The Social Self in Japanese Philosophy and American Pragmatism: A Comparative Study of Watsuji Tetsurō and George Herbert Mead," *Philosophy East and West* 42.3 (July 1992): 475–501; Robert E. Carter, "Interpretive Essay: Strands of Influence" in *Watsuji Tetsurō's Rinrigaku: Ethics in Japan*. Trans. Yamamoto Seisaku and Robert E. Carter, 325–354. Albany: SUNY Press, 1996; Graham Mayeda, *Time, Space and Ethics in the Philosophy of Watsuji Tetsurō, Kuki Shuzo and Martin Heidegger* (New York: Routledge, 2006), particularly chapter 4.
11. For more on the variety of viewpoints in the discussion of Confucian ethics and care ethics see Ranjoo Seodu Herr, "Is Confucianism Compatible with Care Ethics? A Critique," *Philosophy East and West* 53.4 (Oct., 2003): 471–489; Chenyang Li, "Does Confucian Ethics Integrate Care Ethics and Justice Ethics? The Case of Mencius," *Asian Philosophy* 18.1 (2008) 69–82; Xiao Wei, "Caring: Confucianism, Feminism, and Christian Ethics," *Contemporary Chinese Thought: Translation and Studies* 39.2 (Winter 2007): 32–48; Chenyang Li, "Revisiting Confucian Jen Ethics and Feminist Care Ethics: A Reply to Daniel Star and Lijun Yuan," *Hypatia: A Journal of Feminist Philosophy* 17.1 (Winter 2002): 130–140; Lijun Yuan, "Ethics of Care and Concept of Jen: A Reply to Chenyang Li," *Hypatia: A Journal of Feminist Philosophy* 17.1 (Winter 2002): 107–129; Daniel Star, "Do Confucians Really Care? A Defense of the Distinctiveness of Care Ethics: A Reply to Chenyang Li," *Hypatia: A Journal of Feminist Philosophy* 17.1 (Winter 2002): 77–106; Julia Po-Wah Lai Tao,

"Two Perspectives of Care: Confucian Ren and Feminist Care," *Journal of Chinese Philosophy* 27.2 (June 2000): 215–240; Chenyang Li, "The Confucian Concept of Jen and the Feminist Ethics of Care: A Comparative Study " *Hypatia: A Journal of Feminist Philosophy* 9.1 (Winter 1994): 70–89.

12. Mayeda, *Time, Space and Ethics*, 96.

13. See Watsuji, *Ethics*, 89.

14. Watsuji, *Ethics*, 102.

15. Watsuji, *Ethics*, 62.

16. Watsuji, *Ethics*, 62.

17. See Maurice Hamington's *Embodied Care: Jane Addams, Maurice Merleau-Ponty, and Feminist Ethics* (Urbana and Chicago: University of Illinois Press, 2004) for an example of including embodiment as philosophically significant in the Western tradition. While Hamington's book does address embodied care, his framework for philosophy of the body is rooted in phenomenology. As we have seen, what Watsuji's philosophy can add to the theory is significantly different especially regarding the nondualistic concepts of self and bodymind.

18. Kasulis, *Intimacy*, 42.

19. Kasulis, *Intimacy*, 43.

20. Kasulis, *Intimacy*, 42.

21. Kasulis, *Intimacy*, 42.

22. Watsuji, *Ethics*, 66.

23. Watsuji, *Ethics*, 10.

24. Held, *Ethics of Care*, 11.

25. Joan Tronto notes that one requirement of care, along with some kind of engagement, is the following: "First, care implies a reaching out to something other than the self: it is neither self-referring nor self-absorbing," in *Moral Boundaries: A Political Argument for an Ethics of Care* (New York: Routledge, 1993).

26. Takeo Doi, *The Anatomy of Dependence*, trans. John Bester (Tokyo, New York, and San Francisco: Kodansha International, 1973).

27. Doi, *Dependence*, 7.

28. Doi, *The Anatomy of Self*, trans. Mark A. Harbison (Tokyo: Kodansha International, 1985), 34 n.8.

29. Faith Bethelard and Elisabeth Young-Bruehl "Cherishment Culture," *American Imago* 55.4 (1998): 528.

30. Bethelard and Young-Bruehl, "Cherishment," 530.

31. Young-Bruehl, "Where Do We Fall When We Fall In Love?" *Journal for the Psychoanalysis of Culture and Society* 8.2 (2003): 282.

32. Watsuji, *Ethics*, 10.

33. Kazuko Behrens, "A Multifaceted View of the Concept of Amae: Reconsidering the Indigenous Japanese Concept of Relatedness," *Human Development* 47 (2004): 2.

34. Behrens, "A Multifaceted," 15.

35. Behrens, "A Multifaceted," 17. It is important to note that Behrens also demonstrates that wives use *amae* to manipulate their husbands, but the majority of her examples of various kinds of manipulative *amae* do indicate that women are usually the ones being manipulated.

36. Kasulis, *Intimacy*, 118.

37. Kasulis, *Intimacy*, 118.

38. Held, *Ethics of Care*, 39.

39. Held, *Ethics of Care*, 40.

40. Noddings, *Caring*, 86.

41. Held, *Ethics of Care*, 168.

42. Held, *Ethics of Care*, 10.

43. Watsuji, *Ethics*, 124.

44. Held, *Ethics of Care*, 14.

45. See McCarthy, "Ethics in the Between."

46. Held, "Care and Justice in the Global Context," *Ratio Juris* 17.2 (2004): 144.

47. Held, "Care and Justice," 146.

48. Held, *Ethics of Care*, 20.

49. Held, *Ethics of Care*, 21.

50. Held, *Ethics of Care*, 22.

51. Held, *Ethics of Care*, 168.

CHAPTER FIVE

～

Body, Self and Ethics
Watsuji and Irigaray

Moving now to another kind of feminist ethics, we will see how Watsuji's work interacts with that of French feminist philosopher Luce Irigaray. Here we will see that they both have concepts of relational selfhood, view the place of ethics as between people and include the body as a constitutive part of selfhood. Both Watsuji and Irigaray critique the concepts of selfhood, body, and ethics as they have appeared in traditional Western philosophy. Similar to the critique of the West made by defenders of care ethics, they both argue that the view of the self and ethics as dualist and limited leaves us with theories that do not reflect the fullness of human experience in the world. Both Watsuji and Irigaray provide us with alternative, nondualistic models of selfhood. Neither however, on my reading, rejects the notion of the individual; rather, in rejecting the dualisms that permeate Western philosophy they opt for a model according to which *both* individuality *and* relationality are inseparable and equally fundamental to human being-in-the-world.

Watsuji and Irigaray also agree that the body is not merely a contingent aspect of selfhood but integral to it. For them, body cannot be thought of as separate from mind, and it is both an ethical and epistemological site. Watsuji, as we saw in chapter 3, critiques the lack of body in Western philosophy. And Irigaray comes to her concept of the body in large part through a critique of what she sees lacking in the Western philosophical tradition. Both find the vision of ethics and the body in the tradition unsatisfying, as giving us only part of the picture of what it is to be human, much less ethical. While for Watsuji taking the body into account in ethics is a part of being human regardless of gender, Irigaray's work focuses on the female subject. She argues that patriarchy has disembodied the female subject, has not allowed the female as embodied subject to exist, to develop, to flourish, to have a voice. She calls for a "revolution in thought and ethics,"[1] for a carnal ethics, one that "must be constructed or reconstructed."[2] Watsuji's philosophy can provide us with a starting framework, I believe, for constructing such an ethics. Watsuji argues that the very definition of what it is to be human in the West denies the spatiality of the self and as a result leaves out the bodily dimension of being in the world. To summarize, as we saw in chapter 2, Watsuji critiqued Heidegger's *Being and Time*, in particular, for its lack of attention to the spatial aspect of Da-sein. In chapter 3 we discussed the tendency in much of Western thought to treat the human body as merely a material object among others. Watsuji's concept of human being as *ningen* views the body as essential to the notion of the ethical self. We also saw in chapter 3 that Yuasa Yasuo interprets Watsuji's philosophy as building body into his notion of the self and ethics. For both Irigaray and Watsuji then, the body is *not* an object, *not* a mere thing. Rather, the body is a dynamic site, intimately enmeshed with spirit or mind, as well as with other human beings, reaching beyond what we normally consider to be its corporeal boundaries. Through these alternative views of self, we can begin to conceptualize what it is to be an embodied subject and what it means for the encounter with the other(s), which is the requirement, for both philosophers, of ethical being-in-the-world.

Irigaray and Watsuji have two layers of interconnectedness and nonduality at work. Irigaray's work makes an effort to reconnect spirit and body particularly in the female subject. At the same time, her work can be read as imagining a new way of relating between people that is not limited by corporeal boundaries.

The same two levels are present in Watsuji's philosophy of human being as *ningen*. First of all, there is the nondual interconnectedness of mind/body in the individual. Second, he claims this interdependence moves beyond the individual, to interpenetration[3] with other human beings—other bodymind complexes. Watsuji's and Irigaray's concepts of self then, can be brought together to think through ethical being-in-the-world in a way that takes into account the wholeness of being human.

There are important differences, however. Whereas Irigaray's focus is on the re-imagining of selfhood, body and ethics for the female subject, gender concerns do not appear in Watsuji's work. Irigaray not only wants to make a place for the feminine subject but also wants to de-universalize the male subject so that there can truly be a place for both subjects and recognition of difference. Reading Watsuji's work in light of Irigaray enriches Watsuji's view of self, as we will see. However, Watsuji's work can also illuminate Irigaray's since it provides a model of selfhood not based on a dualistic starting point. Irigaray has encouraged this sort of comparison herself having looked at models of the self in the Indian tradition in *Between East and West: From Singularity to Community* and in more recent work. In this chapter, I pursue this suggestion by drawing on Watsuji's work. Reading Watsuji in light of Irigaray reveals, I believe, implications of his work that he did not foresee and these ideas are important because they can help foster understanding across and within genders, nations, cultural and philosophical traditions, in the way Irigaray suggests, and here Watsuji can illuminate ideas in Irigaray's work as well, perhaps in ways she too did not foresee.

Subjects in Betweenness

Irigaray says her philosophy developed through three stages: "the first a critique, you might say, of the auto-mono-centrism of the Western subject; the second, how to define a second subject; and the third phase, how to define a relationship, a philosophy, an ethic, a relationship between two different subjects."[4] Here I explore the third stage of her philosophy by comparing her work with Watsuji's in an effort to clarify the idea of an embodied ethic between subjects.

Irigaray critiques the West for elevating the mind (thus the male subject) over the body (and thus female subject): "Separating body and spirit, he has valorized the one, as the result of a disincarnated speech, making of the other a vehicle, necessary but cumbersome, during existence said to be earthly."[5] According to the tradition she rejects, the body, and more specifically, the female body, is a necessary evil, and there is certainly no cultivation of any relationship between the mind and the body, let alone between men and women. Implicitly also criticizing Descartes' model along similar lines to Leder described in chapter 3, Irigaray states that a "cultivation of breathing, of energy maintains life and health better than abandoning a body-cadaver-animal to medical science and its diverse types of operations."[6] Throughout Irigaray's work, we find her insistence that bodymind must be cultivated if there is going to be understanding between genders, and if we are to ever live ethically in the world.

In *Sexes and Genealogies*, Irigaray maintains that a proper understanding of the feminine "consists in the systematic nonsplit of nature and spirit, in the touching together of these two universals."[7] In other words, Irigaray sees the need for a philosophical recognition of mind (spirit) and body (nature) as integrated in the female subject so as to make questions of the body, and thus of women, central to philosophical reflection. Her work seeks in part to challenge "the dichotomization of the world and knowledge" that, we recall from chapter 3, Elizabeth Grosz argues is a result of the dualisms that are at the foundation of Western philosophy. Irigaray challenges Western philosophy to imagine a concept of self that is not bound by patriarchal or Western frameworks—one that is nondualistic in nature—not built on opposition—but is open to the other and continually becoming, all the while retaining difference. In her philosophy, even though difference is retained, identity is not fixed. It is not fixed because the identity that she imagines for each gender is not oppositional—woman would no longer be identified as that which is not man, she would not be defined in opposition to man, but she would have her own identity and neither woman nor man's identity would be fixed in place for once and for all, for she is a philosopher of change.[8] Irigaray's philosophy aims to inaugurate a truly different subject (woman) and bring her into the philosophical (and political) dialogue. As Tamsin Lorraine describes it, "the implicit assumption of Irigaray's project is that it is more ethical to work toward a cultural imaginary that would support the subjectivity of all through active recognition of our interdependence and mutually constitutive activity than to allow the silencing of an other (or group of others) in order to maintain one's own subjectivity."[9] As Irigaray has shown throughout her work, however, the frameworks of Western, patriarchal philosophies do not provide us with a vocabulary or philosophical framework that is inclusive of both genders.

For Irigaray, subjectivity is embodied. However, despite the fact that the female body is that in which *both* male and female become embodied and the place where selfhood starts,[10] the "womb is never thought of as the primal place in which we become body."[11] Instead we are disembodied—men and women both—for the womb and woman's sexuality becomes a hole, "a devouring mouth" and furthermore representative of all of female sexuality: "The only words we have for women's sexuality are filthy, mutilating words. Consequently, the feelings associated with women's sexuality will be anxiety, phobia, disgust, and the haunting fear of castration."[12] So woman's embodiment, taken over by the language of patriarchy, by the dominant male subjectivity that tries to silence and desubjectivize women, becomes not a place of love, of first intimacy, of creative *puissance*, but a dark, dirty, silent place—a place without a voice, without passion. Irigaray's concept of female subjectivity urges us to "speak the body," to not give it up or give it over to men, to neither deny our embodiment, nor to identify ourselves *only* as maternal bodies in any essentializing sense that would fix a definition of female subjectivity in place for once and for all, but to keep the body as "guardians of the flesh. We should not give up that role, but identify it as our own, by inviting men not to make us into body for their benefit, not to make us into guarantees that their body exists."[13] In reclaiming the body, keeping it as our own, women can re-inscribe the body as an epistemological site. It is important to note that Irigaray is not saying all women need to literally become mothers. The creative *puissance* she urges us to claim as our own can equally importantly give birth to "love, desire, language, art, social things, political things, religious things."[14] Such a view of the female body as creative or productive in itself and not just reproductive, has been systematically denied women from Plato onward, as much feminist literature has shown, and as noted in chapter 3. As Lorraine explains:

> For Irigaray, we need to refuse desubjectivized social roles. The role of the mother is dictated by a social order premised on a division of labor between the producing masculine and the reproducing feminine. In refusing to obliterate the mother's desire in deference to the law of the father, we give her the right to pleasure, sexual experience, passion, and speech. In translating the bond to the mother's body, we discover a language that can accompany bodily experience rather than erase it.[15]

So we begin to imagine a female subjectivity that can, as Irigaray says, "speak the body,"[16] a subjectivity that is embodied but does not trap us in that body. This challenge to speak the body makes a static notion of what it is to be female (or male for that matter) impossible. Such a language, speaking the body, furthermore rejects the mind-body split and creates an adequate language to expresses the fullness of human, lived, embodied experience.

Irigaray's call for philosophical recognition of such fullness echoes the critiques we saw in chapter 3: "development of spirit was presented to me in the form of philosophical or religious texts, of abstract imperatives of (an) absent God(s), at best of politeness and of love. But why could love not come about in the respect and cultivation of my/our bodies?"[17] Female subjectivity, not to mention non-Western philosophical voices, have been left out of the dialogue because of a search for sameness and a silencing of difference. We need a framework that allows for difference without being dualistic (i.e., without privileging one or the other), that provides equal space to *parler-femme* without silencing other voices. A framework that disrupts the traditional notions of what is masculine and what is feminine and that allows for dialogue between the sexes that supports their mutual growth.

Watsuji's notion of self and ethics as *ningen*—which, we recall, literally means "between persons"—provides a framework for imagining and supporting mutual growth and a model of nondual subjectivity. Synthesizing Irigaray's concepts and the directions she points us in with the philosophical vocabulary and concepts of Japanese philosophy can help us, I believe, move even further beyond the binary oppositions that inform patriarchal ways of thinking and seeing the world, to a place where dialogue truly can support mutual growth of human beings, and, hopefully, move us, as a result of understanding between people, out of a culture of violence. As far back as *Sexes and Genealogies* in 1987, Irigaray notes the link between violence and the denial of sexual difference when she states: "We are driven to compete in the rat race of modern life—so maddened and overwhelmed by the pace of existence that we embrace war as a means of regaining some measure of order and opening some new space onto the future. This was often true in the past. It will continue to be so if we fail to set up an ethics of the couple as an intermediary place between individuals, peoples, states."[18]

The core of Watsuji's ethical theory, as we have seen, is his concept of human being understood as *ningen*. We recall that for Watsuji, ethics is the study of human beings, or *ningengaku*: human beings not only as individual but also as social in the betweenness (*aidagara*) among selves in the world at the same time. So Watsuji's view of human being as *ningen* is nondualistic in at least two respects. As we have seen, one such aspect is the nondualism of body-mind; and another is nondualism of self and other, as expressed through his concept of betweenness. Conceptualizing human being as *ningen* argues against the Western concept of self as *purely* individual, where relationships with others are contingent. As we saw in chapter 2, *ningen*'s very structure means that it cannot be thought of as a thing or substance. *Ningen* has, as part of its structure, this sense of reciprocity, a refusal to be a fixed, static object. Its very structure is nondualistic and this nondualism within *ningen*'s structure furthermore mirrors a nondual betweenness with others.

When Irigaray, in *Sexes and Genealogies*, says that we need an ethics of the couple it is a model of interrelationship—or, we might say, of betweenness, of *ningen*—that she has in mind.[19] In *Why Different?*, critiquing the traditional notion of personal identity as self-identity, she articulates her alternative notion of relational identity:

> Relational identity goes counter to this solipsistic, neuter, auto-logical ideal. It contests the cleavages sensible/intelligible, concrete/abstract, matter/form, living/dead. It also refuses the opposition between being and becoming, and the fact that the plural of the one would be the multiple before being the two.

Relational identity considers the concrete identity which is always identity in relation. As such, it is always metastable, becoming. What I try to think is the articulation between the constant transformation required by a living connection to nature and a return to self which permits a being—and a remaining-self in the process of becoming.[20]

Irigaray seeks a concept of self that does not reinforce the identity of sameness. The self, as *ningen* for Watsuji and as seen above for Irigaray, is dynamic, continually becoming; it is not a fixed entity. It is a work in process that is never completed. Watsuji puts it this way: "The subject is not something static like a mirror, whose only business is to contemplate objects, but includes within itself the connections between oneself and the other. And these connections operate subjectively and practically, prior to contemplation."[21] If the subject were static, then relations would be outside of the subject, as on Kasulis's integrity model where "[although] I see myself connected to many other things, none of these things is literally part of me."[22] Human being as *ningen*, however, precludes this. We do not have a notion of relation being one + one + one, where "if *a* and *b* enter into a relation *R*, *a* and *b* are essentially unchanged"[23]—rather relationality, connections are an integral part of human being. For Watsuji, "the standpoint of the isolated subjectivity, which abstracts from the practical connections between person and person, is here forcibly applied to the questions of ethics."[24] To view ethics from such a standpoint is to fail to recognize that, as Irigaray says, lived experience teaches us that the place of ethics is between people, between embodied subjects. And Watsuji suggests that cultivating a concept of human being (*ningen*), if lived, is *inseparable* from ethical being-in-the-world with others.

Bodies in Betweenness

For both Watsuji and Irigaray, connections between people also include corporeal connections—but even this claim requires us to rethink our understanding of the corporeal. Irigaray introduces the idea of the skin or mucous membrane to challenge corporeal boundaries—the idea that our bodies end where our skin ends—and gives us a different way of thinking about interpersonal connections. Attacking binary frameworks that focus on identity as sameness much like Watsuji—but foregrounding that the sameness is a reflection not just of the subject, but of the male subject—she contrasts the notion of the mirror with mucosity. The mirror, she argues, in the same vein as Watsuji, separates self and other—it creates a static image, a reflection of whoever looks into it. In *Speculum*, this is made clear, for the male subject, "in order to assert his own subjectivity . . . must forever distance himself from a feminine and corporeal reality, through a process of deliberate miscognition. Thus, 'mother-matter' must only be 'apprehended by her mirage, not by her dazzling radiance,' in other words, by an image of sameness rather than one of difference: an image that unproblematically *mirrors* masculine identity."[25] Normally, we look into a mirror to see ourselves. Irigaray argues that a result of patriarchy has been that men see their own image even when they look at women, and furthermore that women see a masculine identity even when they look at themselves. In *Sexes and Genealogies*, she comments: "In a way quite different from the mucous membranes or the skin that serve as living, porous, fluid media to achieve communion as well as difference, the mirror is a frozen—and polemical—weapon to keep us apart."[26] Again, the masculine subject, she argues, sees others, even woman, as a reflection of himself. Nonetheless she maintains, even this reflection of himself is seen as other and thus not entering into his identity (contrary to the way a porous membrane is open to and transformed by what is outside it). Binary, polemical frameworks serve to keep us looking outward at the world for sameness, for images that reflect our worldview, for images that reflect ourselves. And if all we find are images of ourselves, they merely reflect and do not transform us. They also overlook differences or reduce them to sameness—to things just like us (or that should be if they are not). And, as Irigaray argues, on the Western philosophical model, regardless of who is looking in the mirror, the self that is both sought and reflected is that of the male subject. And so it becomes the model for what is seen elsewhere. The mirror is static—it merely reflects the person, does not change him or her—it is passive reflection that reflects without modifying or challenging what it reflects—while the mucous membrane, which is porous, allows for interaction with what is apart from it, for relationality in the sense of mutual modification, for coming together as opposed to mere assimilation. Bringing the idea of *ningen* in here, I believe, gives us a way of thinking of selfhood useful for working through the possibilities that Irigaray proposes with the idea of mucous membranes or skin as providing a way of achieving communion or betweenness. As we have little to draw on in terms of conceptual resources or nondualistic philosophical vocabulary in the West, Irigaray struggles to articulate it using metaphors—but Watsuji draws on centuries old concepts behind which are practices—new to us, perhaps, but long established in his tradition. Drawing on him here helps us to articulate what Irigaray is getting at. The mirror is a metaphor for what Edouard Glissant would call a totalizing framework—one that seeks understanding by assimilating difference to what is already understood. It seeks sameness and rest, in the sense of reducing the unknown to the familiar (and comfortable).[27] Dualistic frameworks are totalizing; they leave no room for change or relation with the other, other than in an oppositional framework where one side is devalued. By contrast, Irigaray's metaphor of fluidity and mucosity and Watsuji's concept of *ningen*, not only allow for but promote non-totalizing frameworks. That is, ways of understanding that are open to, and encouraging of, communion with the other (what Glissant calls "Relation") without assimilating or subsuming what is different (i.e., the female) to what is the same (i.e., what is male). The model is not fixed oppositions and permanent categories but rather of relations involving continual and mutual renegotiation and "becoming."

I argued in chapter 3 that even though there is no explicit account of the body in Watsuji, it is clear that it permeates his concept of *ningen* and is central to some of his most evocative examples of betweenness (*aidagara*) and ethics, which, after all, is "concerned with those problems that prevail *between* persons."[28] There I pointed out that Watsuji does not believe that it is possible for people to have either *only* a mental connection *or* only a physical connection. For Watsuji, we know that the body is an inherent part of human being-in-the-world and the body, for him, encompasses human spatiality *and* being-with—being in the betweenness with other human beings. To repeat, he says: "Insofar as betweenness is constituted, one human body is connected with another."[29] In fact, Watsuji insists, we have to work very hard at seeing the body of another person as a mere object. Yet the rising use of rape and sexual assault as "weapons" or tactics in armed conflict speaks to this practice of disembodiment.[30] Here, we see put into action de-personalization and disembodiment—the other is treated as a mere object with no inherent selfhood on the one hand, and on the other, the fact and the way that rape and sexual assault are used as weapons in war speaks to the inseparability of bodymind, as the intent of their use is to assert control *both* physically and mentally on the victims and those around them. To create this way of seeing, involves abstraction from lived reality and we have to *think* our way to such views, rationalize them and work to sustain our view of bodies separate from minds. This attitude runs contrary to our lived, embodied experience of the world. In light of this, it seems there are interpersonal connections—for *ningen* between bodyminds—which go beyond either/or dichotomies (self v. other, body v. mind) and challenge what we normally conceive of as limits of both self and body inasmuch as they cannot be accurately characterized in these terms.

Watsuji and Irigaray are in agreement here, their differences notwithstanding. They each argue for a communion of bodyminds, a concept that has no place in philosophical systems where rationality is privileged and the body ignored or fled from. They insist the body must be understood as rich and complex—as a site for ethical knowledge and for ethics, as involving not just the mind, not just the material body, but both as intimately interconnected as bodymind. As we recall from chapter 3, Watsuji insists that "[w]hen we are aware of something in our mind, this experience already involves the human body as an element within it."[31] It is in this sense that the body is a locus of knowledge. In other words, again we see that concept that we know not just with our minds, but also with our bodies. For Watsuji and Irigaray both, then, to be fully human is to be an integrated human being, a mind-body complex and furthermore to see others as such also. As Tamsin Lorraine states: "A theory of embodied subjectivity can help us map corporeal connections among people and thus indicate how different forms of subjectivity are interdependent and mutually informing. Challenging traditional boundaries among bodies and among minds as well as between bodies and minds allows us to rethink the interdependent nature of subjectivity."[32] Here Lorraine points to what I think we find in both Watsuji and Irigaray (as well as some of what we saw in chapter 4's discussion of the self as found in care ethics).

Bringing together the ideas of Irigaray and Watsuji here we begin to think selfhood in a broader manner—in a way that connects us evermore deeply and differently to other human beings on every level. Realizing that differences between self and other are not entrenched forever, that as we saw in chapter 1 in Kasulis, that knowing we do not understand the other presupposes some basis of understanding, we begin to see that in fact we are much more linked than separated. Thinking this way we realize the potential for broader communion and communication. The work of Irigaray, and as I read him, Watsuji gives us new ideals of human interconnectedness that often get lost in theories of self that focus on the rational and individual. Watsuji's model of human being as *ningen* gives us a structure with which to challenge those boundaries and how we might live, the permeability or porosity of boundaries as one of the very structures of what it is to be human. Thinking about the permeability of corporeal boundaries changes the concept of self as something static or fixed. Drawing on Watsuji and Japanese philosophy here, we can flesh out the analogies Irigaray provides us with and see how such concepts can be lived. As Irigaray proposes, "In this approach, where the borders of the body are wed in an embrace that transcends all limits—without, however, risking engulfment, thanks to the fecundity of the porous—in the most extreme experience of sensation, which is also always in the future, each one discovers the self in that experience which is inexpressible yet forms the supple grounding of life and language."[33] In the "embrace that transcends all limits," two can come together and create a space of betweenness where, even though they are in union, neither subject is engulfed by the other—neither subject loses its identity. This is,

I believe, the same movement of negation inherent in *ningen* that we discussed in chapter 2. Irigaray here recognizes there are differences between (and, I maintain, even within) the sexes, but calls attention to the fact that they are (or should be) complementary—that the "complementarity should be lived in such a way as to facilitate growth."[34] Drawing on Watsuji here, we discover that the male gender has never really been in betweenness with the female gender and that this is impossible so long as gender relations are conceptualized in terms of relations among isolated subjectivities and also so long as female subjectivity is denied by being assimilated to male subjectivity or denigrated because viewed as inferior to male subjectivity. The result is that both genders are prevented from fully understanding and experiencing what it is to be human beings-in-betweenness, and thus, to be truly ethical. As Irigaray puts it:

> The male gender, usually called the human race, plays a game with its other but never couples with it, and ends up by forgetting its gender and destroying its sexual roots. Perhaps it deteriorates and prefers to suffer decline, pain, and death rather than encounter the other.[35]

It is clear that in the above description, an ethics of betweenness is doubly precluded, for not only is there no betweenness of bodymind in the individual, but there is also no encounter, no betweenness with others—which is necessary for ethics.

The other is difficult to encounter because such a meeting involves risk and trust as the quote above implies. After all, what Watsuji and Irigaray demand is a giving over of self, and even though this is only for a moment, the risk and fear are that the other will not take the same risk and one's self will be subsumed by the other—engulfed and lost rather than found. Betweenness gives both genders a place to be openly receptive, both at the same time, yet with the possibility of retaining difference. This difference between genders here is not, I maintain, an essentialism that locks either the male or female subject into one place. I read Irigaray as suggesting that acknowledging such a difference would free both subjects from their current isolated positions.

Irigaray develops this point in her discussion of Descartes' first passion, wonder. She argues that it has been neglected but at the same time suggests a radical re-reading of this notion. She suggests that as a result of the forgetting of wonder, the space between man and woman was filled instead

> with attraction, greed, possession, consummation, disgust, and so on. But not that wonder which beholds what it sees always as if for the first time, never taking hold of the other as its object. It does not try to seize, possess or reduce this object, but leaves it subjective, still free.

> This has never existed between the sexes since wonder maintains their autonomy within their statutory difference, keeping a space of freedom and attraction between them, a possibility of separation and alliance.[36]

Can betweenness provide a space for wonder in this sense . . . a sense of astonishment of beholding something wonderful and new . . . where the female subject is not reduced or possessed by the male subject?

In fact on the betweenness model, the momentary loss of self discussed above—the risk one must take to truly enter into communion with the other—is not necessarily so risky, if it is a part of selfhood, as on Watsuji's *ningen* model—as one would not be subdued, engulfed or possessed. This space of transformation of boundaries is Watsuji's betweenness where the binary oppositions break down—which in turn is the very space of ethics. Practically speaking this does require the loss of self in order to truly be openly receptive in one's response to the other(s)—it is only dangerous it seems to me, when such receptiveness is only on the part of one individual. This is true especially for women but not only for them, as has been the case historically—which is what Lorraine refers to as the "risk of vulnerability to exploitative subjects"[37] and something we need to keep uppermost in our minds as we perform this re-imagining of self. But such opening up to the other, taking the risk to enter into wonder is, I think, necessary for this sort of re-imagining of human subjectivity—of the relationships, the permeability of self/other, male/female, body/mind. Irigaray imagines then, a "couple god" and asks if such a god wouldn't have

> more to say and more, dialectically, yet? No man or woman would achieve absolute knowledge within or according to his or her gender. Each would be constituted in time through a constant articulation between the genders, a dialectic between two figures or incarnations of the living that are represented in sexual difference, and there alone.[38]

Could this be a god or goal of betweenness, one which recognized difference but at the same time the need for a space of coming together that does not involve some form of absolute fixed unity?

The comparison of Irigaray and Watsuji does not stop here. As we saw in chapter 2, the notion of self-negation and contradiction is one of the most complex in Watsuji's philosophy but one which ensures that there is no absolute fixed unity in the space of coming together. Irigaray's idea of the articulation between genders, the preservation of self and other, individual and social, simultaneous with their interpenetration or communion also echoes Watsuji's notion of the human being as *ningen* as continual becoming. In Watsuji, we have seen, becoming is expressed through a movement of negation that he sees as a fundamental structure of the human being as *ningen*. As he sees it, this movement of negation is a process of becoming and links us fundamentally to others. The fundamental structure of *ningen* then, articulates the idea of becoming and remaining self that is central to Irigaray's concept of relational identity. This is clear in her discussion of letting go, in *The Way of Love*, where she writes:

> Releasing all hold would be carried out toward a future of which the equation escapes us, and with regard to an other irreducible to the same for each subject. Letting go then gives access to a truly open space-time where co-belonging is still to be created.[39]

As I read her, this fits with the process of becoming found in *ningen*. However, what Irigaray adds to Watsuji's view is the notion that this would be where *both* the male and female subject could truly come together. She too acknowledges the role of negation in such becoming: "In order to meet with the other, I must first let be, even restore, the nothing that separates us. It is a negative path which leads to the approach of the different and the possible relation with him, or with her."[40] It is betweenness, where, we recall from chapter 2, we find the ground of all distinctions and at the same time discover the nonduality of self and other. If the process of becoming stops—for Watsuji and for Irigaray, the betweenness collapses. If it continues however, as we saw in chapter 2, "the movement of the negation of absolute negativity is, at the same time, the continuous creation of human beings."[41] Watsuji maintains that this is the fundamental structure of our existence—in other words we are constantly, if we are being fully human, becoming.

In *ningen*, the difference between self and other is transcended *yet this transcendence is not a fixed unity*. As we recall from chapter 2, we are both one and many, we are "living self-contradictions" and have individual identities at the same time that we are inextricably interconnected with others. With this kind of mutual negation being a very part of the structure of human being, we gain an increased sense of intimacy with others, or at least become open to the possibility, and there is a never ending reciprocity. As I understand this notion, it is strikingly similar to what lies behind Irigaray's denial of any sense of absoluteness, of fixed universally applicable identities, in her notion of complementarity between genders. In Irigaray's notion of complementarity, there is also a notion of reciprocity, of nondualism at work. Irigaray urges us to move beyond the absolute(s) that Western philosophy would have us believe, for within the absolutes there is no room for such complementarity:

> To want the absolute is not to want those frustrations, privations, temperings that occur when we renounce the immediate for the self so as to secure the work of the negative in the relationship with the other. The absolute knowledge of *one* subject, of *one* gender is in fact the sign that the work of the negative has not been completed.[42]

As I read her, Irigaray is conceptualizing a "negativity" that does not express a lack. Furthermore, she intimates in the final sentence of this quotation, that the work of the negative, and in fact what it is to be *either* male or female is in fact a continuous process—one that is not and should not ever be completed: "The negative that Irigaray has in mind would involve accepting the limits of gender and recognizing the irreducibility of the other. It would thus facilitate a cultivation of the sexed dimension without ever providing it with closure."[43]

Watsuji's self as *ningen*, I believe, allows for thinking the kind of sexual difference that Irigaray advocates.[44] To summarize where we have arrived, Irigaray argues that on the Western philosophical model, there is no betweenness, no genuine encounter with the other. We reduce the other to ourselves for we are caught in the identity of sameness, searching for our own reflection in the other, rather than being open to a true encounter with the other. Both Watsuji and Irigaray agree that we must have a nondualistic concept of self that includes the body and they both agree that we need to rethink relations with the other to adopt an intimacy orientation. Irigaray and Watsuji each enrich the other and potentially give us a new framework, one that provides one way of rethinking relational identity and selfhood as called for by Irigaray.[45] Watsuji gives us the language and conceptual framework that Irigaray seeks through her metaphors and calls to rethink our Western philosophical heritage. Irigaray however, also enriches Watsuji, as his philosophy lacks feminist sensibilities and the implications for gender in his philosophy have not been thought through.

Watsuji's concept of *ningen* and the double negation inherent in *ningen*, gives us a model to begin thinking about this nondualism that allows for difference. As "subjective communal existence," *ningen* is not simply individual + individual + individual; rather, as Watsuji explains, communal relations, "are not objective relations that are established through subjective unity, as is the case with spatial relations between object and object."[46] Human relations, relations between people, require a concept of unity that acknowledges the tension between the two aspects of being human—the individual but understood as always at the same time in relation—and the embodied nature of being human—that Watsuji's theory of *ningen* provides space for *as well as* the tension, the creative tension between genders that Irigaray's feminism rightly insists not be forgotten, not be paved over in the guise of "universality of human beings" or worse, some sort of "neuter" universal. Reading Watsuji, it becomes clear that, while the concept of relationality is certainly foregrounded in looking at ethics, *neither* one of these dimensions of human being-in-the-world is ignored by his theory of *ningen*—and augmenting his philosophy with that of Irigaray ensures that this does not happen. Even the "unity" of betweenness, where the self dissolves into the social is not to be confused with a monism, with something static, for it is always dialectical. Watsuji's model here fits well with Irigaray's, but does not take into account the implications for gender. Both Watsuji and Irigaray advocate for a model that has betweenness but does not dissolve difference—however, Irigaray's model sees the gender implications, that such a betweenness would allow for gender difference to flourish and for each gender to finally have its own subjectivity. She insists that this not be a model by which "the self is equal to *one*"[47] which would dissolve all difference into either one gender (male) or pretend to be neuter and claim an entirely neuter social self, which is what she can add to Watsuji's philosophy. As Watsuji explains, human being as *ningen* involves a "transformation from being to nothingness, and from nothingness to being"[48] *yet without eliminating all differentiation*: "the double negation . . . is not a complete negation that obliterates that which is negated. The identity of self-contradiction makes clear that that which is negated *is preserved*, else there would be no self-contradiction."[49] What Irigaray recognizes but Watsuji doesn't consider is how this preservation of difference can help imagine a new female subjectivity that is not based on dualisms. She urges us to be comfortable with ambiguities as we construct this new subjectivity:

> It would no longer constitute itself in opposition to a self-definition that forms a part of male effectiveness. The female gender, according to the order of its ethical duty, struggles with itself, between light and shadow, in order to become what it is individually and collectively. This growth, which is partly polemical, between conscious and unconscious, immediacy and mediations, mother and women, has to remain open and infinite for and in the female gender. This growth is essential if the two genders are to meet. The greatest fault committed by the race of men was to deprive one gender of its ethical consciousness and of its effectiveness as a gender.[50]

Betweenness, I believe, provides a space for the meeting of genders that is outside of a dualistic framework. What we have seen throughout the last three chapters is that the Cartesian picture does not have the resources to adequately characterize these sorts of interpersonal, corporeal connections and so cannot promote them. On Irigaray's view, as we have seen, promoting such connections and views of self is what needs to be done before we can have an ethics between genders. Watsuji gives us a language for characterizing this experience and thus aids Irigaray's project. Currently, genders are, as she says, "closed up separately in figures of consciousness, of spirit, of race, which allow no passage between them."[51] The "nothingness" aspect of *ningen* is not one in which either male or female gets devoured; rather it is the place where each becomes openly receptive to the other—vulnerable, yes certainly, but this is not just vulnerability on the part of the female subject. Self as *ningen* would be vulnerable to change but not annihilation or conquest or extinction or enslavement. Here, both subjects would be open. This is demanding, for what

> quickly becomes clear is that the structure of existence (*sonzai*) appropriate to human beings (*ningen*) is a mutuality of coexistence that expects and depends on *truth* and *trust* in human relationships. Trust and truth are not intellectual demands made from a purely theoretical interest, but are to be found in the actions of human beings through and by which they are connected with one another. Truth and trust occur spatio-temporally; that is, in the world in which we live as living, breathing, self-conscious bodies.[52]

For Irigaray, the trust and truth that would exist in an ethics of sexual difference are only possible if we can "constitute a possible place for each sex, body, and flesh to inhabit."[53] Such a concept of human being extends well beyond the boundaries of the individual, as well as corporeal boundaries. Cultivating such openness and trust leads to a deepening of relationships. The joy and intimacy that result from a practice of continual mutual transformation through the logic of double negation, through cultivating openness and not seeking absolute identity can then extend even farther, allowing the possibility of genuine dialogue to deepen and, as we saw with care ethics in chapter 4, lead to deeper understanding globally.[54] Living in such a way that we embody this powerful interconnectedness is, I believe, crucial for human flourishing.

Between and Beyond Watsuji and Irigaray

Readers familiar with Watsuji may object that his concept of *ningen* can also be read as undermining difference (precisely what Irigaray rejects and works to overcome in the Western tradition). As John Maraldo explains: "Wastuji writes 'self-other' as a single word (*jita*) that stands on one side of a negative equation whose second side (or negation) is a totality or greater whole. An individual's other half is not really an other individual but the world (*seken*) that makes one a human being. . . . The relevant relationship, for better or worse, is not the relation between self and other."[55] This is certainly true. My response, however, is to ask what prevents us from re-imagining or re-thinking this betweenness where self and other are not separate? Maraldo is right to note that Watsuji puts betweenness above individual and communal, subject and object, self and other—but I have been suggesting that we con-sider betweenness as just one moment in human existence. If we reinterpret Watsuji by infusing his concept with Irigaray's ideas, then I maintain that we will understand the between of the community as a space from which indi-viduals both emerge and return to, transformed in some way by losing self in that between but not necessarily subsuming the other or being subsumed by the other in the process. On this reading, it becomes a space that allows for creative, generative tension or interplay—a place of true communion with the other in a mutual nonhierarchical manner—the possibility that Irigaray aspires to cultivate. On this reading, mindful of Watsuji's description of the continuous movement of negation, one cannot get stuck in the between where one gives over one's self—for it is just a moment in a continual back and forth. This may be, in fact, the sort of transcendence of binary poles Iri-garay is looking for. My suggestion is that by infusing feminism into Watsuji here we can answer Maraldo's critique. Irigaray writes of a transcendence of the other in a relationship (or betweenness) that does not reduce him or her to me or mine. In our encounter with the other, there is wonder: "Awakening us, by their very alterity, their mystery, by the in-finite that they still represent for us. It is when we do not know the other, or when we accept that the other remains unknowable to us, that the other illuminates us in some way, but with a light that enlightens us without our being able to comprehend it, to analyze it, to make it ours."[56] All too frequently, we flee from this strangeness and assimilate the other to ourselves. We get stuck at the pole of individuality and try to secure or "fix" the self in place as a static subject. If, however, we enter into relation in the between, negating in that moment both self and other, this would enact the wonder of the sort that Irigaray seeks. In the between, the other is not reducible to me because, as we saw in chapter 2, there is no other, there is no me, and yet that is at the same time the very root of the differentiation between myself and the other. "Not one, not two" is the way Zen Buddhism expresses this notion, and as Maraldo points out in a discussion of the Ten Oxherding Pictures of Zen Buddhism, it might be that "the conviction that self and other are 'not one and not two' better promotes the very kind of equality the alterists desire. This is not the "'conceit" of equality between real selves' but rather true impartiality."[57] Here there is no hierarchy. Irigaray notes that the "transcendence of the *you* as other is not yet, really, part of our culture. . . . This letting go of the subject, this letting be of the *I* toward what it is, knows, and has made its own, this opening of a world of one's own, experienced as familiar, in order to welcome the stranger, while remaining oneself and letting the stranger be other, do not correspond to our mental habits to our western logic."[58] Bringing Watsuji's structure of *ningen* that both preserves and dissolves oneself in a welcoming of the other allows for the letting go of the subject just cited. She urges us, in much of her work, to not move directly from a celebration of "one" to a celebration of "multiplicity" and calls us to recognize the two—male and female—as subjects in their own rights. She calls us to rethink what being-in-relation is and what its implications are, concluding that this relation has been, in our Western system of thought, in fact unthought—it calls for a different type of thinking.[59] The idea of Watsuji's betweenness and the "not one, not two" of Zen Buddhism that is neither a celebration of multiplicity nor a static absolute is, I believe, one different type of thinking that can cultivate the kind of selfhood, relationality, and ethics that Irigaray seeks. She suggests that one thing necessary for this kind of relational identity to occur is a new model of sexual relations—one that is not about either possessing the other or surrendering oneself to the other. She refers to a "carnal sharing" in love, that love "takes place in the opening to self that is the place of welcoming the transcendence of the other."[60] This place of betweenness, of transcendence, "becomes the place not of a repression or of an exploitation of the flesh but of a poetic, even mystical, progression of love, a path of renunciation of absolute love of oneself with a view to carry out love with the other in the giving up of both self and other, emotionally as well as intellectually. . . . It becomes abandonment to the opening of self and other toward wisdom still unknown."[61] One would come out of such a union, such a communion, altered yet not lost, presumably with a better or transformed sense of self and other but one that requires a moment of dissolution of self and other, a *moment*, perhaps of *jita*. One's individuality, then, can be preserved and yet influenced and mutually informed by an other. It dissolves into community and then reemerges as the individual again, only to resume the process, to continue becoming. If we extend this metaphor of sexual relations through to being-in-the-world as *ningen*, then betweenness provides a model for transcendence of the *you* and the *I* that is embodied and extendable not just to relations within and between genders but even between cultures and philosophical traditions.

Notes

1. Luce Irigaray, *An Ethics of Sexual Difference*, trans. Carolyn Burke and Gillian C. Gill (Ithaca: Cornell U.P., 1993), 6.

2. Irigaray, *Ethics*, 17.

3. I acknowledge that this is a problematic term for feminist philosophy—but it is the term used in the translation of Watsuji's work.

4. Elizabeth Hirsh and Gary A. Olson, "Je—Luce Irigaray: A Meeting with Luce Irigaray," *Hypatia* 10.2 (Spring 1995): 97.

5. Luce Irigaray, *Between East and West: From Singularity to Community*, trans. Stephen Pluháček (New York: Columbia University Press, 2002), ix.

6. Hirsh and Olson, "Je—Luce," ix.

7. Irigaray, *Sexes and Genealogies*, trans. Gillian C. Gill (New York: Columbia U.P., 1993), 112.

8. See Alison Martin, "Luce Irigaray and the Culture of Difference," *Theory, Culture, Society* 20.1 (2003): 1–12.

9. Tamsin Lorraine, *Irigaray and Deleuze: Experiments in Visceral Philosophy* (Ithaca: Cornell University Press, 1999), 21.

10. Lorraine, *Irigaray and Deleuze*, 83.

11. Irigaray, *Sexes*, 16.

12. Irigaray, *Sexes*, 16–17. It is true that there are also such destructive words for male sexuality—and many of our swear words are linked to sex and sexuality. One could argue that neither gender has a healthy sexuality in this sense and Irigaray's re-imagining of female sexuality is a step toward changing attitudes in both genders. I believe, however, that her aim here is to bring our attention to the binary opposition between male and female sexuality that exists. That our attitudes to, and understanding of the sexuality of both genders (whether healthy or not) have been filtered through the male perspective and this has been the standard by which "the other's"—woman's—sexuality has been conceived and measured.

13. Irigaray, *Sexes*, 19.

14. Irigaray, *Sexes*, 18.

15. Lorraine, *Irigaray and Deleuze*, 83.

16. Irigaray, *Sexes*, 19.

17. Irigaray, *Between East and West*, 60.

18. Irigaray, *Sexes*, 5. For a more detailed discussion of how bringing together Irigaray and Watsuji can help promote a sustainable peace see my essay "Towards Peaceful Bodies" in *Philosophieren über den Krieg: War in Eastern and Western Philosophies* (Berlin: Parerga, 2008), 147–164, from which parts of this chapter are drawn.

19. Irigaray, *Sexes*, 5.

20. Luce Irigaray, *Why Different? Interviews with Luce Irigaray*, trans. Camille Collins and ed. Luce Irigaray and Sylvère Lotringer (New York: Semiotext(e), 2000), 159–160.

21. Watsuji, *Ethics*, 31.

22. Kasulis, *Intimacy*, 61.

23. Kasulis, *Intimacy*, 58.

24. Watsuji, *Ethics*, 9.

25. Philippa Berry, "The Burning Glass," in *Engaging with Irigaray*, ed. Carolyn Burke, Naomi Schor and Margaret Whitford (New York: Columbia University Press, 1994), 232. In *Speculum of the Other Woman*, trans. Gillian C. Gill (Ithaca: Cornell University Press, 1985), Irigaray inverts the mirror or the speculum, using the "burning glass" to point the way toward, as Berry states, "a radically new nondualistic mode of physical, metaphysical, ethical speculation" (243). In this work, however, I have chosen to work with the theme that emerges more often after *Speculum*—that of mucosity and fluidity as I find it more useful for challenging the way we think about corporeal boundaries and nondualism.

26. Irigaray, *Sexes*, 65.

27. This kind of relation that supports identity as sameness, as I have argued in more detail elsewhere, is what Glissant would term "totality." See my "Comparative Philosophy and the Liberal Arts: Between and Beyond—Educating to Cultivate Geocitizens," *Canadian Review of American Studies* 38 (2008), and Edouard Glissant, *Poetics of Relation* (Ann Arbor: University of Michigan Press, 2000).

28. Watsuji, *Ethics*, 12. See also my "Ethics in the Between," *Philosophy, Culture, and Traditions* 2 (2003): 63–78, for a more in-depth discussion of this and the discussion of the mother-child relationship in chapter 2.

29. Watsuji, *Ethics*, 68.

30. See the 2006 UN Secretary-General's Report "An In-Depth Study on All Forms of Violence against Women" for more detail on this and other forms of violence against women. It is accessible at http://www.un.org/womenwatch/daw/vaw/.

31. Watsuji, *Ethics*, 66.

32. Lorraine, *Irigaray and Deleuze*, 15.

33. Irigaray, *Sexual Difference*, 18–19.

34. Irigaray, *Sexes*, 107.

35. Irigaray, *Sexes*, 110.

36. Irigaray, *Sexual Difference*, 13.

37. Lorraine, *Irigaray and Deleuze*, 89.

38. Irigaray, *Sexes*, 110.

39. Irigaray, *The Way of Love*, trans. Heidi Bostick and Stephen Pluháček (London and New York: Continuum, 2004), 83.

40. Irigaray, *The Way*, 168.

41. Watsuji, *Ethics*, 117–118.

42. Irigaray, *Sexes*, 110.

43. Lorraine, *Irigaray and Deleuze*, 97.

44. There is more to be said on this topic, though it lies outside the scope of this particular work. The history of power and privilege of patriarchy and the male subject must be taken into account. I am not suggesting here that it would simply disappear if the male subject ascribes to *ningen*. Rather, I am suggesting that *ningen* can provide

a model for establishing female subjectivity. Only after this has been established, however, will the power and privilege of patriarchy disappear.

45. Irigaray, *Why Different?* 162.

46. Watsuji, *Ethics*,18.

47. Irigaray, *Sexes*, 115.

48. Watsuji, *Ethics*, 19.

49. Carter, *Strands of Influence*, 341.

50. Irigaray, *Sexes*, 120.

51. Irigaray, *Sexes*, 121.

52. Carter, *Strands of Influence*, 343.

53. Irigaray, *Sexual Difference*, 18.

54. See Gail M. Schwab's article "Sexual Difference as Model: An Ethics for the Global Future" in *Diacritics* 28.1 (Spring 1998): 76–92, for a study of how Irigaray's ethics can be, as Schwab suggests, "an ethics of difference modeled on sexual difference, an ethics for the future of humanity in all of its diversity" (76).

55. John Maraldo, "Between Individual and Communal, Subject and Object, Self and Other: Mediating Watsuji Tetsurō's Hermeneutics," in *Japanese Hermeneutics: Current Debates on Aesthetics and Interpretation*, ed. Michael F. Marra (Honolulu: University of Hawai'i Press, 2002), 84.

56. Irigaray, *Between East and West*, 123.

57. John Maraldo, "Alterity and Nonduality in the Oxherding Pictures of Chan/Zen" (unpublished paper presented at the American Academy of Religions, Buddhism Section, November 2000).

58. Irigaray, *Between East and West*, 125.

59. Irigaray, *The Way*, 90–91.

60. Irigaray, *Between East and West*, 115.

61. Irigaray, *Between East and West*, 116.

CHAPTER SIX

Conclusion

Throughout this book I have argued for the transformative potential of comparative feminist philosophy. I first articulated the striking similarities that exist between certain strands of Japanese philosophy and feminist philosophy concerning selfhood, ethics and the body. I then explained the differences between these philosophies and pointed out how each signals limitations in the other. Finally, I urged on the basis of this sort of constructive comparison a view of ethical selfhood that goes beyond where each of these views leaves us when it is considered in isolation. The critical comparison I have offered not only illuminates complexities in each of these philosophies; it provides clues about how to live the model of selfhood, ethics, and the body that has emerged through this encounter.

There remains, however, the vital task of putting these ideas to work. If we take the view I have presented in this book seriously, we cannot simply re-imagine selfhood and ethics from a purely conceptual standpoint. One of the most important lessons to emerge from my comparison is that taking both feminist philosophy and Japanese philosophy seriously requires not only the cultivation of certain ideas but of the way of life they envision. Indeed, understanding the view I promote requires enacting the new way of being-in-the-world that I have tried to articulate. The new way of thinking about ethics and the self is to be embodied in a new way of living. The hope is that by cultivating more porous boundaries between self and other, embracing the interdependency and interconnectedness of human being-in-the-world and rethinking what it is to be a self, we will be more open in our encounters with others and truly meet them, on the model of *ningen*, in the between. Although far easier said than done, this would represent an enormous step toward mutual understanding and equality in the world.

As I see it, cultivating the sort of understanding that is integral to the view I promote is an urgent task. In war-torn parts of the world, violence seems to increase daily: Iraq, Chad, Darfur, Afghanistan. Soldiers and civilians, men, women and children fall prey to acts of violence that turn our stomachs.[1] Who can forget the images of Iraqi prisoners abused in Abu Ghraib prison, or charred corpses of American soldiers dragged through the streets of Fallujah? (Never mind the unimaginable horrors we are not permitted to see.) And then there are images of a war of sorts that we are less commonly shown—images of violence against women that occur, not only in Africa and the Middle East during times of war, but in "peaceful" and "secure" nations. Even in our own neighborhoods, women are silenced and denied their subjectivity in a very real way. Who cares for them?

At a fundamental level, we have a visceral, corporeal reaction to these various sorts of violence as wrong, unethical things that simply shouldn't be happening. We physically want to turn away; we search for explanations and may even cling to justifications of collateral damage and other attempts at sense making to help us sleep without nightmares. Yet in our "guts"—in a place in our bodies all too easily ignored—we know that what we see is wrong, repulsive, unethical and ought not to be—despite the best efforts to explain or justify it. Faced with images of blackened eyes, bruised flesh, bloody bodies and torn limbs, we cannot—certainly not without enormous effort—separate body from mind—the immediate reaction to these images is one lived in bodymind. In that moment, we react as a whole human being—our judgments and reactions are fused and embodied.

Cultivating the kind of selfhood I have been promoting in this book, is a matter of cultivating and honoring the kind of understanding and empathy that comes out of listening to our bodyminds, as well as cultivating and honoring our interconnectedness with other bodyminds. This view brings the bodymind into philosophy as a source of wisdom and love that can no longer be dismissed. Cultivating this kind of selfhood connects us more deeply to those who suffer—whether they live close to home or far away, as my analysis of Watsuji, Irigaray, and care ethics reveals.

In bringing Japanese and feminist philosophy into dialogue, and reevaluating the place of the body in ethical selfhood, I have urged that when ethics is embodied it has implications that are transnational, transcultural and universal in the best sense of the term. By this I mean that cultivating a notion of embodied ethical selfhood means connecting human beings deeply to one another and providing a basis for cross cultural dialogue and understanding, while at the same time creating a space for the recognition of, and respect for, differences. This is a very different ideal than the sort of universality that flattens out differences under the guise of false claims to neutrality or the conflation of what is truly universal with what is merely Western (or Eastern) or male (or female). It is also very different from resigning oneself to Huntington's notion of an inevitable "clash of civilizations."[2] These latter two ideals preclude the possibility of genuine cross-cultural understanding. Creating spaces for real dialogue, founded in care and communion that respect difference, also gives us, as we saw in the discussion of Irigaray, a foundation for the female subject—a foundation that is her own as opposed to simply being a reflection of the male subject which is still the dominant subjectivity. In bringing continental philosophy, Watsuji, care ethics and Irigaray together in dialogue, I have also taken up the challenge of making philosophy "radically plural."[3] Encouraging the ability to see problems, people, our own place in the world from a multiplicity of perspectives—in line with the view I have been advancing—can go a long way to realizing equality among cultures and genders, of respecting and supporting everyone's subjectivity.

In thinking about ways to advance the ideas I have been exploring, a natural place to turn is education. In many ways, liberal education is still under the seventeenth century humanist ideals on which it was founded—ideals which reflect Kasulis's description of the integrity orientation discussed in chapter 1.[4] As feminist scholar bell hooks observes, in *Teaching to Transgress*, the academy has traditionally forced us to think of ourselves dualistically—to carve out a distinction between the intellectual and the emotional, the mind and the body—and encourages the separation of our "professional" intellectual lives and our personal or private lives. She states that "the objectification of the teacher within bourgeois educational structures seemed to denigrate the notion of wholeness and uphold the idea of a mind/body split, one that promotes and supports compartmentalization."[5] hooks explicitly encourages "the intellectual questing for a union of mind, body and spirit."[6] As she emphasizes, pursuing this vision *does not* mean checking one's intellectual or critical faculties at the door. To the contrary, the aim is to recognize, as I have discussed in connection with Yuasa and feminist philosophy, that purely intellectual questing, as traditionally conceived, is partial and the goals of education—including the development of intellect—can better be advanced by cultivating bodymind in the classroom in order to achieve the full development of our students. hooks contends that as professors, "our work is not merely to share information, but to share in the intellectual and spiritual growth of our students. To teach in a manner that respects and cares for the souls of our students is essential if we are to provide the necessary conditions where learning can most deeply and intimately begin."[7] In my own career, I initially resisted this view of teaching. Teaching, as I conceived it when I started, was about engaging intellectually with my students, but I balked at accepting what I viewed then as a "maternal" role, fearing that this diminished my authority in the classroom as an intellectual and that it even infantilized my students. I did not see that caring "for the souls of my students" does not mean compromising myself or them as intellectuals (or as people) and in fact enhances intellectual development (both theirs and mine). Teaching in a liberal arts university for a decade has led me to reject my former, dualistic approach to teaching, reevaluate my connection to students and stop thinking about my teaching in a dualistic manner that involved separating the intellectual from the subjective and embodied. As I now see it, fostering nondualism and taking care are integral to the intellectual development of my students. They are essential to my teaching and encourage compassion, relatedness and ethics in my students (and in me).

Cultivating ways of teaching, learning and, thus, thinking that challenge dualistic ways of understanding and being-in-the-world—in the way I have been suggesting in light of notions developed by Watsuji and Irigaray and in care ethics—is a risky endeavor. It requires teachers and students alike to face new complexities in the classroom, complexities that are at times difficult to navigate. Challenging dualisms requires both me and my students to embrace ambiguities not always expected in a university classroom setting and to accept that there are not necessarily well-defined answers to problems, such as the answers and problems that we find in dualistic frameworks.

hooks asks us to focus on building community, creating "a climate of openness and intellectual rigor."[8] Putting into practice what I have urged in this book can help foster such a community. One important way to put the ethical embodied self into practice is by teaching comparative feminist philosophy. As a teacher, I challenge my students' assumptions about what is "East" and "West"; what is "male" and "female"; what "knowing" something means; what "self" means. I challenge their tendencies to privilege one discourse over another simply because it is more familiar, while at the same time teach them that certain discourses and ways of knowing, such as patriarchy, *have* been privileged arbitrarily, while other voices have been unjustly silenced.[9] At the same time, I also challenge their tendency to abrogate critical reflection by endorsing all discourses as on a par. So teaching the views about ethical, embodied selfhood I have been discussing throughout this book and the kind of change in living one's life that it demands is one way to cultivate the kind of feminist cultural change I have been advocating. I put the philosophy into practice by putting the practice into philosophy.

In searching for ways to promote the ideals developed in this book outside the confines of academic philosophy, I am encouraged by the new direction in liberal education being pursued in contemplative education. At its most basic level, contemplative education proposes the integration of Asian contemplative practices into methods of higher education.[10] While the ins and outs of contemplative education defy easy summary, it is helpful to consider however briefly, the kind of classroom it sets out to foster.

Contemplative education aims to enhance learning of all subjects, not just philosophy or ethics. As Harold Roth, director of Brown University's Contemplative Studies Initiative, observes: "current North American higher education is dominated by what we might call third-person learning. We observe, analyze, record, and discuss a whole variety of subjects at a distance, as something 'out there,' as if they were solely objects and our own subjectivity in viewing them does not exist."[11] The comparative feminist philosophical investigation I have engaged in here has revealed that this kind of approach to knowledge is neither necessary, nor desirable and that it will only ever lead to partial understanding. As feminist philosophy teaches, we all bring our subjectivity to the classroom and bring it to bear on learning even in the purest intellectual endeavors. As feminist standpoint epistemology has shown us, in particular, ignoring this dimension of learning or investigating has resulted in oppression and the silencing of voices.

According to Roth, contemplative education "reenvision[s] certain basic aspects of the existing models of teaching and research in higher education in order to foster a deeper knowledge of the nature of our existence as human beings in a world that is intricately interrelated on many levels."[12] This suggests that contemplative education holds promise as a way of fostering the comparative feminist philosophical project I have engaged in this book, while adding new dimensions to it. On the model of self I have defended, human beings are intricately interrelated with one another and the world around them. By integrating a comparative feminist philosophical perspective with techniques of contemplative education, education can better foster the development of the subjectivity of all students in the classroom—women and men alike—and promote the embodiment of the ethics that, I have argued, is central to both Japanese philosophy and feminist philosophy.

Contemplative education acknowledges that we all learn from a particular standpoint, one that affects both our teaching and learning. As we have seen, if self is relational as Watsuji, Irigaray and care ethics contend; if we embrace the nondualism of self and other; if we have the trust Watsuji promotes as well as the openness Irigaray advocates, then there is more of a chance that the sort of community that hooks advocates—the equality that Irigaray and care ethics advocate and the ethics that Watsuji advocates—will find a place to grow and flourish. Attending to the personal dimensions of learning encouraged by both contemplative education and feminist philosophy does not mean that we find ourselves in a classroom, where the professor surrenders her expertise on the subject matter at hand. Nor does it mean that the classroom becomes a space for indulging in narcissistic musings untethered from the subject matter and texts. Nor still does it mean denying difference or the fact that power differentials between teacher and student exist. The suggestion is rather that all parties involved acknowledge that they are each part of the learning process—that each has a different approach and life experience and each is responsible for what happens in the classroom, and that these various voices and experiences do enter into the classroom and learning that takes place. This requires a true meeting of bodyminds in the classroom—an important step, I am convinced, in meeting hooks' challenge of creating an environment of "openness and intellectual rigor" through fostering the kind of self I have been arguing for. In contemplative education, both teacher and student are required to be fully present and participatory in the classroom. While this may well happen unconsciously or inadvertently in traditional classrooms, in contemplative education this coming together and being present is *consciously* and deliberately cultivated through the use of embodied practice. The relational self that we have seen in Watsuji, Irigaray, care ethics, and the vision of liberal education articulated by hooks challenges—and even demands—that we bring more of our and our students' subjectivities into the classroom without—although this presents one of its biggest challenges—turning the classroom into a free-for-all therapy session. The point is not to denigrate intellectual learning, theory or third-person analysis and critique, but rather to recognize that a pedagogy that takes the whole self into account enhances and supplements the goals and ideals of liberal arts education that have been passed down through the centuries. It also means integrating body and mind in contexts in which the body has been neglected, or viewed simply as a tool—something that is non- or even anti-intellectual. Teaching on this model requires a different approach than is currently the norm. My suggestion here is that contemplative education provides a promising starting point for future work.

Perhaps a couple of anecdotes will render this suggestion more concrete and show both the need for the kind of embodied ethical selfhood I have been arguing for and some idea of the ways in which embodied practice can help teach it. I recently taught a course entitled "Buddhism, Meditation and

Identity" in which I was able to combine some aspects of contemplative education with some of the subject matter of this book. In addition to reading classical and contemporary texts on Buddhism, meditation, and identity, we also had a one-hour meditation lab every week where we embodied the practices we were reading about. In addition to this, students were required to commit to practicing for twenty minutes a day whichever meditation technique we were studying that week. I was open with the students about the fact that this was the first time I had taught this course and that I was curious to see if doing the embodied practices of meditation would help them understand the philosophical concepts better. One of the most interesting discussions we had in this course, however, and one that I did not expect, was about the Metta, or "loving-kindness," meditation. This is one of the oldest Buddhist meditations and comes out of the Theravada tradition. One begins by offering loving-kindness, peace, well-being and happiness to oneself and then after several weeks of practice opens the meditation outward, to someone significant in one's life—perhaps a good friend or mentor—then to one's family, then strangers and then the whole universe. What struck me in teaching this to my students and discussing it with them afterwards was not only that this meditation was the one they found most difficult but that what they found most difficult about it was offering such a meditation to themselves. Despite the rugged individualism encouraged in North American society and the stress on individualism and autonomy in the tradition of liberal education, my students were extremely uncomfortable wishing *themselves* loving-kindness, happiness, peace and well-being. This strikes me as something of a paradox. In a North American society that celebrates individualism, these individuals were struggling to be kind to themselves or self-regarding. How can we expect them to be compassionate towards others—to feel connected to others both near and far, to share or even recognize the suffering of others or injustice—if they cannot in this very simple way, feel connected to themselves? For me, the contrast between the image of people as "looking out for number one" and yet unable to be kind and compassionate to themselves, speaks to the need for shifting the concept of selfhood away from the isolated individual to the relational self. As I see it, such a shift would go a long way to help students feel connected to both themselves and others. Nor does it seem to me to be an accident that the need for fostering this kind of selfhood was brought into sharp relief by having students undertake an embodied practice. Their understanding of themselves and of the philosophical ideas was evident in their bodily experience. The result was much deeper knowledge and a much richer experience than simply learning about this meditation in a lecture or discussion. The students lived and breathed the struggle and emerged with a deepened understanding of compassion and loving-kindness.

At the end of the semester, students universally agreed that practicing the various kinds of meditation as they learned about them greatly advanced their understanding of Buddhist concepts such as emptiness and non-self for example. Indeed, I was struck that the conversations about emptiness and non-self were quite different in this class from other courses in which we did not do any embodied practice. Allowing students to bring their own experience of meditation to our discussion, significantly improved the level of understanding. The lecture/discussion model I had previously relied on, when I might have dropped in a sample meditation once or twice a semester, has not been nearly as effective as the incorporating of regular embodied practice into lectures and discussions. While this evidence is largely anecdotal, the experience encourages me to explore further ways of incorporating embodied practices into my teaching to help students better learn the subject matter.

I also believe, partly on the strengths of results with contemplative education, that cultivating this kind of selfhood does not need to be confined to courses in which embodied practice is the subject at hand. By way of offering practical tools for fostering the sort of change in the classroom I envisage, I suggest two very rudimentary techniques—rooted in Asian traditions—that might be applied in any classroom, regardless of the subject matter. In the spring semester of 2009 I was fortunate to spend the semester at Naropa University as a Lenz Foundation Residential Fellow. During this time, I had a chance to see contemplative education in action firsthand, as it is the governing teaching philosophy at Naropa. Almost every meeting at Naropa starts with a bow—this is a non-religious ritual that signals the coming together of the community for whatever purpose—be it a class (on whatever subject), an assembly, a celebration or even a faculty meeting. As it was explained to me, the purpose of the bow is to help everyone be present—to give the best part of themselves to the task at hand and to honor the other people involved in it. There are three distinct aspects to the bow, even though it only takes a moment to perform. First one "holds the space"—one sits up straight, hands on thighs, looking ahead and/or at those in the class or meeting (often in a circle); next, one "feels the space"—the surrounding community, opening up to whatever will occur in the class or meeting; and finally one "gives" to those in the room the actual bow.[13] While hardly a panacea, this very simple act of embodied contemplation can be used in any classroom as a means of setting the tone, reminding those present of where they are, why they are there, and encouraging everyone to come together in common purpose. The aim is to better connect people and build community by fostering the sense of interdependence, openness and trust—crucial elements for fostering relational selfhood.

An alternative embodied practice is to simply sit in a moment of silence together before launching into a class—to perform a mini-meditation, as it were. In my classes I have found this helps focus both students and me on the work we are about to embark on together.

To some, such simple techniques will seem hokey or contrived. Yet they can easily be performed and even with students with no interest in, or knowledge of, Buddhism or spirituality, they serve to cultivate a different atmosphere in the classroom, one that in my experience enhances learning. We are not used to doing much of anything embodied in classrooms—and these simple techniques—the bow, a minute or two of meditation or mindfulness—feel terribly awkward and contrived at first—but their effect is palpable. My experience is that students and teachers feel as though they are being a bit silly or making fools of themselves—but I have found if I trust that the students will follow my lead, that for the most part, everyone tries it. We all feel foolish or silly together at first, but soon enough it becomes a part of the rhythm of the class. This creates trust among the classroom community—and in other classes where I have started with a moment of meditation or mindfulness, I have yet to receive any negative feedback—most students in fact comment that they quite like it—that it helped ground them and get them ready for class and if I happen to forget and try to rush right into the subject matter, they remind me that we haven't done our meditation yet.

No one is suggesting these techniques in themselves will transform liberal arts education, much less the culture at large. My point in introducing them was rather that for all their simplicity, these techniques can direct both students and teachers to connect to one another and, moreover, can encourage the realization—in the sense of "making real" or embodying—the interconnectedness we all share. We are individuals, to be sure, and certainly unique, *yet at the same time*, as we have seen, we are deeply interdependent and it takes all of us together to create an atmosphere where engaged, deep, embodied learning takes place—whether it is through learning math or philosophy or feminism or Buddhism. These simple techniques are offered merely as a reminder that we are not just minds in the classroom, but bodyminds in the world. They are intended to help us realize and remember Yuasa's comment that learning with the mind only is only partial learning. Even these simple efforts in embodied practice, require us to be vulnerable and to enter into a relationship of trust, as both Watsuji and Irigaray have noted.

The model of comparative feminist contemplative education I am imagining, requires that students not be passive in their learning and education.

It asks them to engage in the classroom learning in a deeper way than they might usually engage. In contemplative education, using critical first-person introspection with an eye to bringing increased openness to both the subject matter and the community in which students study avoids the narcissism that people often fear when they hear it suggested that subjectivity should be brought into the classroom. In contemplative education, students are required to take a critical first-person perspective. That is, their self-reflection is connected to their mastery of the subject matter and its purpose is to serve a deeper understanding of both the individual student and what he or she is learning. It is anything but free-floating introspection. We are deeply interconnected to others around us as well as the subject matter we study and teach and these interconnections, as we have seen articulated in both feminist and Japanese philosophies, go beyond our families, classrooms, institutions and out into the entire universe. The program of cultivating self-hood through education that I am envisioning aims to make space in liberal education for empathetic, compassionate and ethical being-in-the-world. But it has to begin from a place within the individuals who engage in this work—teachers and students alike.

Even with such simple techniques as outlined above, I believe, the payoff can be vast and far reaching. Further developing ways of living interconnectedness and ways to foster it in our classroom by integrating the principles I have been discussing throughout this work into learning at all levels and with all kinds of people is an enormous challenge, but also, I think, a very promising avenue to pursue.

Notes

1. I leave out the case of those who derive pleasure rather than horror when faced with such events—and wish to engage in harnessing the notion that we are all embodied beings for ethical purposes, and ultimately, although this will be the subject of future work, for greater cross cultural understanding. Hence, I do not address in depth the issue of how the body is used, for example, in torture.

2. Samuel Huntington, *The Clash of Civilizations and the Remaking of World Order* (New York: Simon & Schuster, 1996).

3. See James Heisig, "Redefining Philosophy: An Apology for a Sourcebook in Japanese Philosophy," in *Japanese Philosophy Abroad* (Nagoya: Nanzan Institute for Religion and Culture, 2004).

4. For more on this, see Erin McCarthy, "Comparative Philosophy and the Liberal Arts: Between and Beyond—Educating to Cultivate Geocitizens," *Canadian Review of American Studies* 38.2 (2008): 293–309.

5. bell hooks, *Teaching to Transgress: Education as the Practice of Freedom* (New York and London: Routledge, 1994), 16.

6. hooks, *Teaching to Transgress*, 16.

7. hooks, *Teaching to Transgress*.

8. hooks, *Teaching to Transgress*, 40.

9. See McCarthy, "Comparative Philosophy."

10. For more on contemplative education see http://www.naropa.edu/conted/index.cfm and http://www.acmhe.org/. Also see *Teachers College Record* 108.9 (September 2006), which was devoted to the topic of contemplative education.

11. Harold Roth, "Contemplative Studies: Prospects for a New Field," *Teachers College Record* 108.9 (September 2006): 1790.

12. Roth, "Contemplative," 1800.

13. See http://www.naropa.edu/about/bow.cfm for a more detailed explanation of the bow and its history.

Bibliography

Behnke, Elizabeth. "Edmund Husserl's Contribution to the Phenomenology of the Body in *Ideas II*." *Issues in Husserl's Ideas II*. Ed. Thomas Nennon and Lester Embree, 135–160. Dordrecht: Kluwer, 1996.

Behrens, Kazuko. "A Multifaceted View of the Concept of *Amae*: Reconsidering the Indigenous Japanese Concept of Relatedness." *Human Development* 47(2004): 1–27.

Bethelard, Faith, and Elisabeth Young-Bruehl. "Cherishment Culture." *American Imago* 55.4 (1998): 521–542.

Carter, Robert E. "Introduction to Watsuji Tetsurō's *Rinrigaku*." In *Wastuji Tetsurō's Rinrigaku: Ethics in Japan*. Trans. Yamamoto Seisaku and Robert E. Carter, 1–6 (Albany: SUNY Press, 1996).

———. "Watsuji Tetsurō" in the *Stanford Internet Encyclopedia of Philosophy*, http://plato.stanford.edu/entries/watsuji-Tetsurō/#Bib.

———. *Encounter with Enlightenment: A Study of Japanese Ethics*. Albany: SUNY Press, 2001.

Cornwell, Grant, and Eve Walsh Stoddard. "Peripheral Visions: Towards a Geoethics of Citizenship." *Liberal Education* 89.3 (Summer 2003): 44–51

Dilworth, David, and Valdo H. Viglielmo with Agustin Jacinto Zavala. "Chapter Four: Watsuji Tetsurō." In *Sourcebook for Modern Japanese Philosophy*. Westport: Greenwood Press, 1998.

Doi, Takeo. *The Anatomy of Dependence*. Trans. John Bester. Tokyo: Kodansha International, 1973.

———. *The Anatomy of Self*. Trans. Mark A. Harbison. Tokyo: Kodansha International, 1985.

Drummond, John. "The 'Spiritual' World: The Personal, the Social, and the Communal." In *Issues in Husserl's Ideas II*, 237–254. Dordrecht: Kluwer, 1996.

Fynsk, Christopher. *Heidegger: Thought and Historicity*. Ithaca: Cornell University Press, 1986.

Gilligan, Carol. *In a Different Voice: Psychological Theory and Women's Development*. Cambridge: Harvard University Press, 1982.

Glissant, Edouard. *Poetics of Relation*. Ann Arbor: University of Michigan Press, 2000.

Grosz, Elizabeth. *Volatile Bodies: Toward a Corporeal Feminism*. Bloomington: Indiana University Press, 1994.

Heidegger, Martin. *Being and Time*. Trans. Joan Stambaugh. Albany: State University of New York Press, 1996. Translation of *Sein und Zeit*, 17th ed. Tübingen: Max Niemeyer Verlag, 1993.

———."Building Dwelling Thinking." In *Poetry, Language Thought*. Trans. Albert Hofstadter, 143–162. New York: Harper and Row, 1971.

Heisig, James. "Redefining Philosophy: An Apology for a Sourcebook in Japanese Philosophy." In *Japanese Philosophy Abroad*. Nagoya: Nanzan Institute for Religion and Culture, 2004.

Held, Virginia. *The Ethics of Care: Personal, Political, and Global*. New York: Oxford University Press, 2006.

———. "Care and Justice in the Global Context." *Ratio Juris* 17.2 (2004): 141–155.

Hirsh, Elizabeth, and Gary A. Olson. "Je—Luce Irigaray: A Meeting with Luce Irigaray." *Hypatia* 10.2 (Spring 1995).

Husserl, Edmund. *Cartesian Meditations*. Trans. Dorion Cairns. The Hague: Martinus Nijhoff, 1967. Translation of *Cartesianische Meditationen und Pariser Vorträge. Husserliana*, vol. 1., 2nd ed., ed. S. Strasser. The Hague: Martinus Nijhoff, 1973.

———. *Ideas Pertaining to a Pure Phenomenology and to a Phenomenological Philosophy: Second Book: Studies in the Phenomenology of Constitution*. Trans. R. Rojcewicz and A. Schuwer. Dordrecht: Kluwer, 1989. Translation of *Ideen zu einer Reinen Phänomenologie und Phänomenologischen Philosophie: Zweites Buch: Phänomenologische Untersuchungen zur Konstitution. Husserliana*, vol. IV. Ed. Marly Biemel. The Hague: Martinus Nijhoff, 1952.

Irigaray, Luce. *An Ethics of Sexual Difference*. Trans. Carolyn Burke and Gillian C. Gill. Ithaca: Cornell University Press, 1993.

———. *Between East and West: From Singularity to Community*. Trans. Stephen Pluháček. New York: Columbia University Press, 2002.

———. *Sexes and Genealogies*. Trans. Gillian C. Gill. New York: Columbia University Press, 1993.

———. *Why Different? Interviews with Luce Irigaray*. Trans. Camille Collins, ed. Luce Irigaray and Sylvère Lotringer. New York: Semiotext(e), 2000.

———. *The Way of Love*. Trans. Heidi Bostick and Stephen Pluháček. London: Continuum, 2004.

Kasulis, Thomas. *Zen Action/Zen Person*. Honolulu: University of Hawaii Press, 1981.

———. "Editor's Introduction" to *The Body: Toward an Eastern Mind-Body Theory*, by Yuasa Yasuo. Albany: SUNY, 1987.

———. *Intimacy or Integrity: Philosophy and Cultural Difference*. Honolulu: University of Hawaii Press, 2002.

King, Sallie. "Egalitarian Philosophies in Sexist Institutions: The Life of Satomi-san, Shinto Miko and Zen Buddhist Nun." *Journal of Feminist Studies in Religion* 4 (1988): 7–26.

Lafleur, William R. "Buddhist Emptiness in the Ethics and Aesthetics of Watsuji Tetsuro." *Religious Studies* 14 (1978): 237–250.

Leder, Drew. "A Tale of Two Bodies: The Cartesian Corpse and the Lived Body." In *Body and Flesh: A Philosophical Reader*, ed. Donn Welton. Oxford: Blackwell, 1998.

Lorraine, Tamsin. *Irigaray and Deleuze: Experiments in Visceral Philosophy*. Ithaca: Cornell University Press, 1999.

Loy, David. *Nonduality: A Study in Comparative Philosophy*. New Haven: Yale University Press, 1988.

Maraldo, John. "Watsuji Tetsurō Ethics: Totalitarian or Communitarian?" In *Komparative Ethik: Das gute Leben zwischen den Kulturen*, ed. Rolf Elberfeld and Günter Wohlfart. Köln: edition chōra, 2002.

———. "Between Individual and Communal, Subject and Object, Self and Other: Mediating Watsuji Tetsurō's Hermeneutics." In *Japanese Hermeneutics: Current Debates on Aesthetics and Interpretation*, ed. Michael F. Marra. Honolulu: University of Hawai'i Press, 2002.

———. "Alterity and Nonduality in the Oxherding Pictures of Chan/Zen" (unpublished paper presented at the American Academy of Religions, Buddhism Section), November 2000.

Martin, Alison. "Luce Irigaray and the Culture of Difference." *Theory, Culture, Society* 20.1 (2003): 1–12.

Mayeda, Graham. *Time, Space and Ethics in the Philosophy of Watsuji Tetsurō, Kuki Shuzo and Martin Heidegger*. New York: Routledge, 2006.

McCarthy, Erin. *The Spatiality of the Self*. Ph.D. dissertation, University of Ottawa, 2000.

———. "The Knowing Body." In *Sagesse du corps*, ed. Gabor Cspregi. Aylmer: Éditions du Scribe, 2001.

———. "Ethics in the Between." *Philosophy, Culture, and Traditions* 2 (2003): 63–78.

———. "Towards Peaceful Bodies." In *Philosophieren über den Krieg: War in Eastern and Western Philosophies*, 147–164 Berlin: Parerga, 2008.

———. "Comparative Philosophy and the Liberal Arts: Between and Beyond—Educating to Cultivate Geocitizens." *Canadian Review of American Studies* 38.2 (2008): 293–309.

———. "Towards a Transnational Ethics of Care." In *Frontiers of Japanese Philosophy II: Neglected Themes and Hidden Variations*, ed. Victor Hori and Melissa Curley. Nagoya: Nanzan Institute for Religion and Culture, 2008.

Nagami, Isamu. "The Ontological Foundation in Tetsurō Watsuji's Philosophy: *Kū* and Human Existence." *Philosophy East and West* 31.3 (July 1981).

Nagatomo, Shigenori. Review of "Watsuji Tetsuro, *Watsuji Tetsuro's Rinrigaku: Ethics in Japan*." *The Eastern Buddhist* 30.1 (1997): 152–158.

———. "Translators Introduction." In *The Body, Self Cultivation and Ki-Energy*, by Yuasa Yasuo. Trans. Shigenori Nagatomo and Monte S. Hull. Albany: SUNY Press, 1993.

Nagatomo, Shigenori, and Gerald Leisman. "An East Asian Perspective of Mind-Body." *The Journal of Medicine and Philosophy* 21 (1996).

Noddings, Nel. *Caring: A Feminine Approach to Ethics and Moral Education*. Berkeley: University of California Press, 1984.

Roth, Harold. "Contemplative Studies: Prospects for a New Field." *Teachers College Record* 108.9 (September 2006): 1787–1815.

Schwab, Gail M. "Sexual Difference as Model: An Ethics for the Global Future." *Diacritics* 28.1 (Spring 1998): 76–92.

Shaner, David Edward. *The Bodymind Experience in Japanese Buddhism: A Phenomenological Study of Kūkai and Dōgen*. Albany: SUNY Press, 1985.

Spelman, Elizabeth. "Woman as Body: Ancient and Contemporary Views." *Feminist Studies* 8.1 (Spring 1982).

Theunissen, Michael. *The Other: Studies in the Social Ontology of Husserl, Heidegger, Sartre, and Buber*. Trans. Christopher Macann. Cambridge, Mass.: MIT Press, 1984.

Tronto, Joan. *Moral Boundaries: A Political Argument for an Ethics of Care* (New York: Routledge, 1993).

United Nations. 2006 UN Secretary-General's Report. "An In-depth Study on All Forms of Violence against Women."

Watsuji, Tetsuro. *Climate and Culture*. Trans. Geoffrey Bownas. New York: Greenwood Press, Inc. in cooperation with Yushodo Co., Ltd., 1988.

———. *Watsuji Tetsuro's Rinrigaku: Ethics in Japan*. Trans. Yamamoto Seisaku and Robert E. Carter. Albany: State University of New York Press, 1996.

Young, Iris Marion. *On Female Body Experience: "Throwing like a Girl" and Other Essays*. Oxford: Oxford University Press, 2005.

Young-Bruehl, Elizabeth. "Where Do We Fall When We Fall in Love?" *Journal for the Psychoanalysis of Culture and Society* 8.2 (2003): 279–288.

Yuasa Yasuo. *The Body: Toward an Eastern Mind-Body Theory*. Trans. Nagatamo Shigenori and T. P. Kasulis. Albany: State University of New York Press, 1987.

———. "Cultivation of the Body in Japanese Religions." Trans. Shigenori Nagatomo (unpublished essay given to the author by Yuasa in 2001).

———. *The Body, Self Cultivation and Ki-Energy*. Trans. Shigenori Nagatomo and Monte S. Hull. Albany: SUNY Press, 1993.

——. "Sexuality and Meditation." (Unpublished paper given to the author).

——. "A Contemporary Scientific Paradigm and the Discovery of the Inner Cosmos." In *Self as Body in Asian Theory and Practice*. Ed. T. P. Kasulis, R. Ames and W. Dissanayake. Albany: SUNY Press, 1993.

Zaner, Richard. *The Problem of Embodiment: Some Contributions to the Phenomenology of the Body*. The Hague: Martinus Nijhoff, 1964.

Index

authenticity, 17, 21–25

becoming, 18, 24, 26, 46, 76, 78–79, 81, 85, 90
being-with, 20–23, 81
betweenness (*aidagara*): ethics of, 49, 58, 81, 83; Irigaray and, 75, 78–79, 80, 82–87, 89, 90; Watsuji and, 13, 16, 18, 23, 25, 28–29, 33, 36, 39–43, 58, 60, 78, 81, 84, 87–90
body, xiii–xiv, 1–3, 4, 36, 60, 82, 96, 97, 100, 104n1; Buddhism and, 37, 48; care ethics and, 59, 62, 65, 67; feminist philosophy and, 37–39; Husserl and, 33–36; Irigaray and, 4, 73–79, 82, 88; *ningen* and, 39–44; Watsuji and, 59–60, 73–74, 81–82; Western philosophy and, 36–37, 41, 43, 46, 48; Yuasa and, 38, 44–50. *See also* somatic
bodymind, 4, 37–41, 43–50, 96; contemplative education and, 97, 100, 103; Irigaray and 75, 83
Buddhism, 1, 11, 17, 37, 45, 46–47, 48, 55, 64, 89, 90, 101

comparative philosophy, x, xiv, 1, 66–68
contemplative education, 8, 99–104

difference, xiii, 3, 5, 15, 75–78, 80, 83, 84, 86–88, 97, 100
dualism, 6, 15, 17, 34, 39, 41, 47–48, 73, 76, 87

empathy, 5, 6, 43, 61, 96
emptiness: Buddhist, 15, 17–18, 102; *ningen* and, 16–17, 25, 29, 43, 48. *See also* negation

feminism, 1, 3, 64, 68, 87, 89, 103

gender, xi, xii, xiv, 3, 66, 68, 74–76, 83–88, 90, 91n12, 97
Gilligan, Carol, x, 4, 56–57
Grosz, Elizabeth, 37–38, 46, 76

Heidegger, Martin, x, 1, 6, 11–12, 20–26, 27, 30, 43, 57, 74
Held, Virginia, x, 7, 57–58, 61, 63–69
hooks, bell, 97–98, 100

Husserl, Edmund, 6–7, 12, 26–30, 33–36, 39, 40, 43, 57

individualism, xiii, 12, 15, 56, 64, 101
integrity, 3–6, 29, 36, 55–58, 63–64, 79, 97
interdependence, x, xi, xiii, 5, 16, 17, 27–28, 37, 43, 55, 57–59, 61–62
intersubjectivity, 7, 12, 26, 33, 57
intimacy, xi, 3–8, 14, 16, 26, 36, 40, 55–56, 60, 63, 76, 85–86
Irigaray, Luce, x, xi, 2, 4–5, 8, 16, 19, 73–90

Kasulis, Thomas P., 3–8, 14, 16–17, 26, 29, 36, 50, 55, 60, 62–63, 79, 82, 97

Lorraine, Tamsin, 9n9, 76, 77, 82, 84

Maraldo, John, 13, 89

negation: Buddhism and, 15–16; Irigaray and, 82–83, 85; ningen and, 16–19, 24–25, 29, 39, 43, 46, 85–88, 89. See also emptiness
ningen, 6–7, 12–20, 23–26, 28–29, 33, 39–44, 47, 49–50, 56–58, 60–61, 63, 65, 74, 78–79, 80–90, 92n44, 96
Nishida Kitaro, xi, 11, 15, 46, 48, 49, 52n32
Noddings, Nel, 4, 56–58, 64–65
nondualism, 15, 20, 35, 38, 43, 50, 53n71, 65, 78, 85–86, 92n25, 98–99

somatic, xi, xii, 3–4, 36, 60. See also body
spatiality, 12, 23–25, 34–35, 74, 81

Yuasa Yasuo, 7, 9n9, 38, 39–41, 43, 44–50, 74, 97

About the Author

Erin McCarthy is Associate Professor of Philosophy at St. Lawrence University where she also teaches in the Asian Studies Program. She is the author of several articles in both French and English in the fields of pedagogy, ethics, and comparative feminist philosophy. Professor McCarthy has served on the board of ASIANetwork in various capacities since 2006, including Chair for 2009–2010.

CPSIA information can be obtained at www.ICGtesting.com
Printed in the USA
267940BV00003B/13/P

9 780739 120507